Junior MasterChef

OFFICIAL RECIPE COLLECTION

Paste your photo here

Hello

There's no doubt that the standard of cooking on Junior MasterChef surprised everyone who watched, which is why putting together this recipe collection was something of a challenge. Of course we wanted to feature the best recipes from the show, but we also wanted to create a guide for the vast majority of kids who aren't quite up to recreating George and Gary's prawn tortellini with marron and pumpkin purée just yet! So you'll find everything here, from Isabella's gnocchi to Stephanie Alexander's leg of lamb, plus really easy dishes such as vanilla biscuits and mango ice blocks. Everything's been tried and tested in the MasterChef Magazine kitchens, so you're guaranteed success every time. Have fun!

Trudi

Trudi Jenkins
Editor-in-chief
MasterChef Magazine

Contents

getting STARTED

Congratulations to Isabella on being named the first ever Junior MasterChef!

CHOPPING BOARDS

* Chopping boards can be made of wood or plastic.
* Place a tea towel under your board to prevent it slipping while chopping.
* Keep boards clean by washing them with water and dishwashing liquid, then drying with a towel.
* Always wash boards after cutting meat or fish on them, or if they've come in contact with raw egg.

LESSON 1
Hygiene

✳ Make sure your hands are clean. Always wash them with soap and warm water before you start cooking and don't dry wet or sticky hands on your clothes – use a clean tea towel or paper towel.
✳ Always scrub your nails before and after cooking.
✳ Before you start, remove any jewellery.
✳ Tie your hair back – no one likes to find a runaway hair in their dinner!
✳ Wear an apron (or clothes you don't mind getting dirty!) to ensure you don't stain your clothes.

KNIFE NOTES

Surprisingly, a blunt knife is more dangerous than a sharp knife. With a blunt knife, you have to apply more pressure to cut through food, so if the knife slips, you could cut yourself badly. With a sharp knife, very little pressure is needed to glide through food, so any mishaps are likely to result in a small cut. For the safest techniques, see right.

LESSON 2
Cutting techniques

BRIDGE If it's a hard, round or awkwardly shaped item, ask an adult to cut it in half first. Form a bridge with the thumb and index finger of one hand and hold the item on a chopping board with the flattest part down. Hold a knife in the other hand and position the blade under the bridge, then cut downwards firmly.

CLAW Place the flat side of the item you want to cut down on the chopping board. Shape the fingers of one hand into a claw shape, tucking the thumb inside the fingers. Rest the claw on the item to be sliced. Holding the knife in the other hand, slice the item, moving the clawed fingers away as the cutting progresses.

Pumpkin Soup with Honeyed Croûtons

SERVES **12**
PREPARATION **20 MINS**
COOKING **50 MINS**

This makes a big batch of soup. Store it in the fridge for up to 3 days, or divide it into portions and freeze them for up to 2 months.

1.2kg butternut pumpkin
2 tbs olive oil
2 red onions
4 carrots
2 red capsicums
1 tbs vegetable stock
powder

MY SCORE /10

STEP 1

Preparing the pumpkin

Preheat oven to 180C. Using a large sharp knife, cut the pumpkin in half lengthwise. (You will need an adult to help you.) Using a tablespoon, scoop out seeds and discard. Using a pastry brush, brush pumpkin flesh with 1 tbs olive oil. Place the pumpkin, cut-side down, on an oven tray. Roast in the oven for 25 minutes.

STEP 2

Preparing the onion

While the pumpkin is cooking, using the bridge technique (see Lesson #2, page 7), cut the onions in half from top to bottom, leaving the roots intact. Peel and discard the skin, then cut the onions into thin wedges.

Chef's tip To reduce the stinging effect of the onion on your eyes, rinse the onion halves after peeling them.

STEP 3

Chopping the vegetables

Using the claw cutting technique (see Lesson #2, page 7), cut off the root end and top of the carrots. Using a vegetable peeler, peel carrots, then cut in half lengthwise using the bridge technique. Then, using the claw technique, cut the carrots into small pieces. Using the bridge technique, cut capsicums in half lengthwise. Remove seeds and, using the claw technique, cut into pieces. Place onions, carrots and capsicums in a bowl, add remaining 1 tbs olive oil and mix with your hands.

STEP 4

Roasting the vegetables

Using oven gloves, carefully remove the hot tray from the oven. Add the vegetable mixture to the tray, then return to the oven and roast for a further 25 minutes or until the vegetables are soft. Carefully remove the hot tray from the oven. Test the pumpkin with a skewer; it should feel soft. Set aside to cool. When the pumpkin is cool enough to handle, cut into large pieces using the bridge technique. Peel skin and, using the claw technique, chop into small pieces.

STEP 5

Blending the vegetables

Place half the roasted vegetables in a blender. Ask an adult to help you do this. Add 600ml water and 2 tsp stock powder. Cover with the lid. Blend vegetables until smooth, adding a little more water if mixture is too thick. Transfer soup to a saucepan, then repeat blending with remaining vegetables, 600ml water and the remaining 2 tsp stock powder. Warm the soup in the saucepan over medium heat and serve with honeyed croûtons (see below).

Honeyed croûtons

Preheat oven to 200C. Using the bridge and claw cutting techniques, cut 2 bread rolls into cubes. Place the bread on an oven tray and drizzle with 2 tbs honey and 1 tbs olive oil. Bake the bread for 6–8 minutes or until golden. Remove and set aside to cool. Serve the honeyed croûtons with soup. Serves 6.

Chicken Pita Pockets

MY SCORE /10

MAKES 4
PREPARATION 15 MINS

4 x 17cm pita bread rounds
2 small green or
   red apples
2 carrots
½ lemon, juiced
2 stalks celery
2 barbecued skinless
   chicken breasts or
   8 slices ham
25g (¼ cup) roughly
   chopped walnuts
35g (¼ cup) Craisins*
   or raisins
75g (¼ cup) mayonnaise
2 tsp honey
10 mint leaves, torn

Who needs cutlery?
Wrap chicken and
crunchy coleslaw in
pita bread, pick up
and tuck in – perfect
for school lunches!

STEP 1
Preparing the pita bread
Place one pita bread flat on a chopping board or a clean work surface. Hold it down with one hand, tucking your thumb under your fingers. Using a sharp paring knife, carefully cut a slit along the edge furthest away from your hand to make a pocket. Repeat with the remaining pita.

STEP 2
Preparing the apples
Using the bridge technique (see Lesson #2, page 7), cut the apples in half. Using a melon baller, scoop core from the centre. Using the bridge technique, cut each half lengthwise into 2 pieces. Or you can quarter the apples, then place the wedges on their sides. Using the claw technique (see Lesson #2, page 7), cut out the core.

STEP 3
Grating the carrots and apples
Using a vegetable peeler, peel carrots. Using a box grater, hold the top of the grater firmly with one hand. With your other hand, hold a carrot at the top end of the grater and push down the side of the grater with the largest holes. Repeat with the remaining carrot and apple quarters. Transfer the grated apples and carrots to a large bowl. Add 1 tbs lemon juice and toss to combine. (Adding lemon juice will stop the apples turning brown.)

STEP 4
Preparing the filling
Using the claw technique, cut the celery into thin slices. Using your hands, tear the chicken into long, thin shreds or, if using ham, roughly chop the ham with a large knife. Add chicken to the apple mixture, then add walnuts and Craisins, and stir to combine. To make the dressing, place the mayonnaise, honey and remaining lemon juice in a small bowl. Add the mint and, using a large spoon, stir to combine.

STEP 5
Making the pockets
Add the dressing to the chicken mixture and stir to combine. Add freshly ground black pepper, tasting to check the flavour. Using a large spoon, spoon equal amounts of mixture into the pita pockets. Place them on individual plates to serve, or seal in snap-lock bags and take them to school in a cooler bag or chilled lunch box.
✳ Craisins is a brand of dried, sweetened cranberries available from supermarkets.

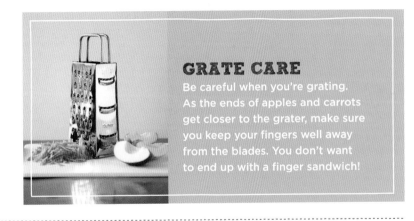

GRATE CARE
Be careful when you're grating. As the ends of apples and carrots get closer to the grater, make sure you keep your fingers well away from the blades. You don't want to end up with a finger sandwich!

Super Smoothies

Berry smoothies
SERVES **2**
PREPARATION **15 MINS**

250g (1 punnet)
  strawberries
1 tbs honey
250g (1 cup) frozen
  berry yoghurt
500ml (2 cups) milk
200g (1½ cups) fresh
  or frozen raspberries

Using a knife, hull the strawberries (remove the green tops), then place in a blender with the honey, yoghurt, milk and 1 cup raspberries. Cover with lid, then blend until smooth. Pour the smoothie into 2 glasses and serve topped with remaining raspberries.

Chef's tip When measuring honey, spray the spoon with cooking oil spray – this helps the honey slide straight off.

Mango & passionfruit smoothies
SERVES **2**
PREPARATION **15 MINS**

5 passionfruit
1 mango
2 scoops frozen
  mango yoghurt
2 tbs desiccated coconut
1 tsp vanilla extract
125ml (½ cup) coconut milk
375ml (1½ cups) milk

Cut passionfruit in half and remove pulp. Set aside 1 tbs pulp to serve. Cut mango into cubes (see Lesson #25, page 129). Place passionfruit, mango, yoghurt, coconut, vanilla, coconut milk and milk in a blender. Cover with the lid, then blend until smooth. Pour the smoothie into 2 glasses and serve topped with reserved passionfruit.

Caramel & banana smoothies
SERVES **2**
PREPARATION **15 MINS**

2 bananas, chopped
2 scoops vanilla ice-cream
2 tbs caramel topping
30g (¼ cup) malted
  milk powder
500ml (2 cups) milk
Pinch ground
  cinnamon

Place the bananas, vanilla ice-cream, caramel topping, malted milk powder and milk in a blender. Cover with the lid, then blend until smooth. Pour the smoothie into 2 glasses and serve with a sprinkle of ground cinnamon.

Add porridge oats to a smoothie to make a healthy breakfast on the go!

MY SCORE   /10

Masterclass with Stephanie
Meatballs with Flatbreads and Carrot Salad

SERVES 6
PREPARATION 45 MINS
COOKING 30 MINS

1 tbs extra virgin olive oil, plus extra, to brush
150g (1 cup) plain flour, plus extra, to dust
1 tbs finely chopped rosemary
15 English spinach leaves
200g plain yoghurt
2 tsp cumin seeds
2 tsp coriander seeds
1 tsp paprika
2 tbs roughly chopped flat-leaf parsley
2 tbs chopped coriander
½ onion, chopped
500g minced beef
1 lemon, zested
12 x 8cm rosemary sprigs, most leaves removed to make skewers
40g butter, melted

Carrot salad
2 carrots, peeled, grated
2 tbs extra virgin olive oil
½ lemon, juiced
1 tbs chopped flat-leaf parsley
1 tbs chopped coriander
2 tbs pistachios
2 tbs sultanas
2 drops rosewater

STEP 1
Making the flatbreads
To make flatbreads, combine oil and 125ml (½ cup) warm water in a jug. Place flour, rosemary and ½ tsp salt in a food processor, cover with the lid, then process until combined. Slowly pour in oil through the feed tube (get an adult to help you) and process to a soft dough. Transfer dough to a floured surface and knead until smooth. Place in a bowl, cover with plastic wrap and set aside for 30 minutes.

STEP 2
Making the carrot salad
For the carrot salad, combine all ingredients in a bowl. Season, then set aside until ready to serve.

STEP 3
Making spinach yoghurt
To make the spinach yoghurt, heat 2 tbs water in a large frying pan over medium-high heat. Add the English spinach leaves, then cook, stirring, for 2 minutes or until wilted. Drain the spinach (get an adult to help you), then cool. Once cool, squeeze the spinach to remove excess liquid, then roughly chop. Combine spinach and yoghurt in a bowl. Season, then set aside until ready to serve.

STEP 4
Making the meatballs
Heat a frying pan over medium heat. Add cumin and coriander seeds, and cook, stirring, for 2 minutes or until fragrant. Transfer to a mortar, then pound with a pestle to a fine powder. Stir in paprika. Place herbs, onion, beef, zest and spices in a food processor. Cover, then process to a smooth paste. Transfer to a bowl. Season. Brush an oven tray and rosemary skewers with oil. Squeeze 2 tablespoons mince around each skewer to form a ball. Brush mince with oil and place on tray. Repeat to make 12 skewers. Heat a chargrill pan over medium-high heat. Cook skewers for 8 minutes, turning, or until browned and cooked through. Transfer to a clean tray, then rest for 5 minutes.

STEP 5

Cooking the flatbreads

Preheat oven to 100C. Line an oven tray with foil. To finish the flatbreads, divide the dough into 12 balls, then roll out each portion on a lightly floured surface until very thin (about 3mm). Heat a large frying pan over medium heat and dry-fry the bread (without any oil), in batches of 2, for 3 minutes on each side or until golden. Transfer flatbreads to the lined oven tray, brush with melted butter, then keep warm in the oven until ready to serve. Serve the meatballs with the flatbreads, carrot salad and spinach yoghurt.

✳ Rosewater is water that's distilled with rose petals. It's from delis and Middle Eastern grocers.

MY SCORE   /10

*Perfectly cooked prawns,
lovely flavours – well done!*

MATT PRESTON

MY SCORE   /10

Anthony's
Garlic Prawns

SERVES **4**
PREPARATION **10 MINS**
COOKING **15 MINS**

2 slices sourdough bread
80ml (⅓ cup) olive oil
6 cloves garlic,
   thinly sliced
2 small red chillies, seeds
   removed, finely chopped
1kg large green prawns,
   peeled with tails intact,
   cleaned (see Lesson #11,
   page 53)
½ cup basil leaves,
   finely shredded
Crusty bread and lemon
   wedges, to serve

STEP 1 Preheat oven to 180C. Remove the crusts from the bread, then roughly tear bread into pieces. Place bread in a food processor, cover with the lid (get an adult to help you), then whiz until you have coarse breadcrumbs.
STEP 2 Spread the breadcrumbs over a small oven tray, then bake for 5 minutes. Using oven gloves, remove the tray from the oven, then give the breadcrumbs a stir (get an adult to help you). Bake in the oven for a further 5 minutes or until dry, but not coloured. Set aside to cool.
STEP 3 Heat oil in a large frying pan over medium–high heat. Add the garlic and chilli, and cook, stirring, for 30 seconds. Add the prawns and cook, turning, for 4 minutes or until just cooked.
STEP 4 Add the breadcrumbs and basil, and cook for 1 minute or until combined and well coated. Season to taste with salt and pepper, then serve with crusty bread and lemon wedges.

ABOUT ANTHONY

At 10 years old, Anthony, from New South Wales, was one of the competition's youngest contestants. His fabulous garlic prawns blew the judges away in Heat Four of the Top 50. "These prawns are creamy, crunchy and very tasty – you're an absolute star," said Anna Gare.

about
EGGS

To centre the yolks for hard-boiled eggs, start stirring the eggs for 3 minutes once the water comes to a simmer. When you quarter the eggs, the amount of white around the yolk will be evenly distributed.

LESSON 3
Poaching eggs

STEP 1

Working with one egg at a time, crack an egg into a small cup. Fill a deep frying pan or wide saucepan with water until about 8cm deep. Add 2 tsp white vinegar and 1 tsp salt. Bring to the boil over medium–high heat. Reduce heat to low–medium – the water should be just simmering. Fill a bowl with cold water and set aside. Using a wooden spoon or whisk, stir the simmering water in one direction to create a whirlpool (this will help to give your poached eggs a neat shape).

STEP 2

Working in batches of two, slide the egg from cup into centre of whirlpool, as close to water as possible, then repeat with a second egg. Without stirring, cook eggs for 2½ minutes for a semi–soft yolk or 3½ minutes for a firm-set yolk. Using a slotted spoon, transfer the eggs to the bowl of cold water (this stops the cooking process). Remove with a slotted spoon, then drain on a plate lined with paper towels. During the cooking, scoop any foam from the water surface with a slotted spoon. Repeat with remaining eggs.

LESSON 4
Boiling eggs

Place room temperature or refrigerated eggs in a saucepan. Run cold water into the pan until the water is 2cm above the eggs. Place pan over medium–high heat and bring to the boil. Reduce heat to a simmer and set your timer for 4 minutes for soft-boiled eggs or 9 minutes for hard-boiled eggs.

Potato & Vegetable Frittata

SERVES **6**
PREPARATION **15 MINS**
COOKING **30 MINS**

4 small floury potatoes
   (such as coliban), peeled
6 eggs
2 tbs olive oil
1 large red onion
175g baby spinach,
   washed, drained
40g (⅓ cup) grated
   cheddar cheese

MY SCORE   /10

*Frittatas are great as you can fill them
with almost any vegetables, cheeses
or meats you have on hand. Frittatas
also travel well – in Italy, people take
wedges to school or work for lunch.*

STEP 1
Preparing the potatoes and eggs

Place potatoes in a small saucepan, cover with water, bring to the boil, then cook for 15 minutes or until just tender. Drain and cool. Using the bridge technique (see Lesson #2, page 7), cut potatoes in half, then into 1cm slices. Crack eggs into a large bowl. Using a fork, whisk together, then season with salt and pepper.

STEP 2
Preparing and cooking the vegetables

Peel and halve the onion (see Skill 1, below). Using the claw technique (see Lesson #2, page 7), thinly slice onion (you may need an adult to help with this). Heat the oil in a large ovenproof frying pan over gentle heat. Add the onion and cook for 10 minutes, stirring occasionally, or until the onion is soft. Add potato slices and spinach to the pan and cook for 2 minutes or until spinach has wilted, stirring very carefully so that you don't break up the potatoes.

STEP 3
Cooking the frittata

Preheat grill to high. Pour the egg into the frying pan and stir gently so that the egg covers the base of the pan. Reduce heat to low and cook the frittata for 3 minutes or until the egg is almost set and only a little runny egg is left on top.

STEP 4
Finishing the frittata

Sprinkle cheese over the frittata, then carefully transfer the pan to the grill and cook for 5 minutes or until set and top is golden. Remove the pan from the grill (get an adult to help). Cool slightly, then cut into wedges to serve.

SKILL 1 Peeling onions

Using the bridge technique, cut the onion in half lengthwise. Place the 2 halves, cut-side down, on the chopping board. Slice off the unusable portions at the top and bottom of each half. Peel back the papery top layer of each onion half, then rinse under cold water to remove any remaining skin, as this can cause eyes to water.

Masterclass with Anna
Mexicana Omelette

MAKES 2
PREPARATION 30 MINS
COOKING 10 MINS

For smaller appetites, cut the omelette in half and serve 4, or keep for lunch the next day.

6 eggs
2 tbs milk
2 pinches smoked
   Spanish paprika
80ml (⅓ cup) olive oil
½ x 400g can kidney
   beans, rinsed, drained
½ small red onion,
   finely chopped
½ vine-ripened tomato,
   seeded, finely chopped
100g shaved ham,
   roughly torn
60g thinly sliced edam*
Crème fraîche or sour
   cream and coriander
   leaves, to serve

Avocado salsa
½ Lebanese cucumber
1 long red chilli
1 avocado, chopped
   (see Chef's Tip)
1 tbs lemon juice
1½ tbs olive oil

STEP 1
Making the salsa
Using the bridge technique (see Lesson #2, page 7), cut the cucumber and chilli in half lengthwise. Using a small spoon, scoop seeds from cucumber and chilli. Discard seeds. Using the claw technique (see Lesson #2, page 7), cut the cucumber, chilli and avocado into long thin strips, then cut into cubes. Place the avocado, cucumber and half the chilli in a bowl. Add lemon juice and olive oil to the salsa, then season with salt. You won't need any pepper because of the chilli. Using a spoon, gently stir ingredients together to combine, then set aside.

STEP 2
Making the omelette
Crack the eggs into a jug. To do this, firmly tap the side of the egg on the edge of the jug, then, using both hands, pull the shell and away allow the egg to drop into the jug. Add the milk, paprika and a pinch of salt to the jug, then, using a whisk or fork, beat until well combined. Heat 2 tbs olive oil in a 20cm omelette pan or non-stick frying pan over low heat. Pour in half the egg mixture.

STEP 3
Filling the omelette
Cook the omelette for 1½ minutes or until it begins to set at the edges. Scatter with half each of the kidney beans, onion, tomato, ham, cheese and half the remaining red chilli from the salsa. Cover with a lid, a sheet of foil or a plate (get an adult to help you), then cook for a further 4 minutes or until the egg is set and the cheese has melted.

Chef's tip Cut avocado in half lengthwise around the middle, then, using a spoon, scoop out the seed. Cut halves into quarters, then peel away skin. Cut avocado into cubes.

STEP 4

Serving the omelette

Using oven gloves or a tea towel, remove the lid (get an adult to help you). Holding the handle, ease a spatula around the side of the pan, then, holding the pan at an angle, slide the omelette onto a plate. Repeat with remaining oil, egg, beans, onion, tomato, ham, cheese and chilli to make a second omelette. Serve omelettes topped with crème fraîche, salsa and coriander.

✳ Edam is a Dutch semi-hard cow's milk cheese available from supermarkets. Substitute cheddar or a more flavoursome cheese such as provolone or gruyère.

MY SCORE   /10

Chillies are hot, so always wash your hands well after touching them. Be careful not to rub your eyes when handling them or they will sting!

Masterclass with Stephanie
Bacon & Egg Pie

SERVES **6**
PREPARATION **20 MINS**
COOKING **45 MINS**

This recipe is taken from Stephanie Alexander's *The Cook's Companion* (Penguin/Lantern). You will need to allow 1 hour to make and rest the pastry before rolling it out.

1 quantity shortcrust pastry (see recipe, page 92)
Cooking oil spray
6 rashers thickly sliced streaky bacon, rind removed
2 tbs chopped flat-leaf parsley
1 tsp freshly snipped chives
11 eggs

STEP 1
Lining the tart pan
Using cooking oil spray, grease a 22cm tart pan with a removable base. Cut pastry in half. Roll out 1 half of the pastry on a lightly floured piece of baking paper to 3mm thick. Roll pastry up around the rolling pin, then gently unroll it over the tart pan. Working quickly, ease pastry into corners. There will be excess pastry at the top of the tart. Using scissors or a knife, trim pastry, leaving a 1cm border (this will allow for shrinkage during cooking). Place tart shell in freezer for 20 minutes for the pastry to rest. Roll out second piece of pastry in the same way as the first, until 24cm round. Place on a tray in the fridge.

STEP 2
Cooking the bacon
Heat a non-stick frying pan over medium heat. Lightly spray the pan with oil (get an adult to help), then cook the bacon, stirring frequently with a wooden spoon, for 8 minutes or until golden and lightly crisp. Drain on a plate lined with paper towel.

STEP 3
Filling the tart shell
Remove the tart shell from the freezer. Scatter two-thirds of the bacon over the base of the tart shell. Scatter with half the herbs. Break 10 of the eggs (see Lesson #20, page 91), one at a time, into a cup and carefully slip each into the pastry case, being careful not to break the yolks. Season with salt and pepper, then scatter with remaining herbs and bacon.

Chef's tip Some cooks pierce the yolks after putting the eggs in the tart shell, to achieve a more 'layered' pie.

STEP 4
Baking the tart
Meanwhile, preheat oven to 180C. Cover the pie with the second pastry round. Let the pastry settle over the hump of each egg, then trim it and seal the edges carefully. Whisk the remaining egg and a pinch of salt together in a small bowl, then brush over pastry. Bake for 35 minutes or until the pastry is a rich golden colour. Cool in the pan for 10 minutes before slicing and serving warm or cold.
∗ Streaky bacon is the tail end of the loin (it does not contain the eye) and is often known as belly bacon or kaiserfleisch.

MY SCORE   /10

Resting pastry helps relax the gluten in the flour and gives the pastry a better texture. It also helps to reduce shrinkage.

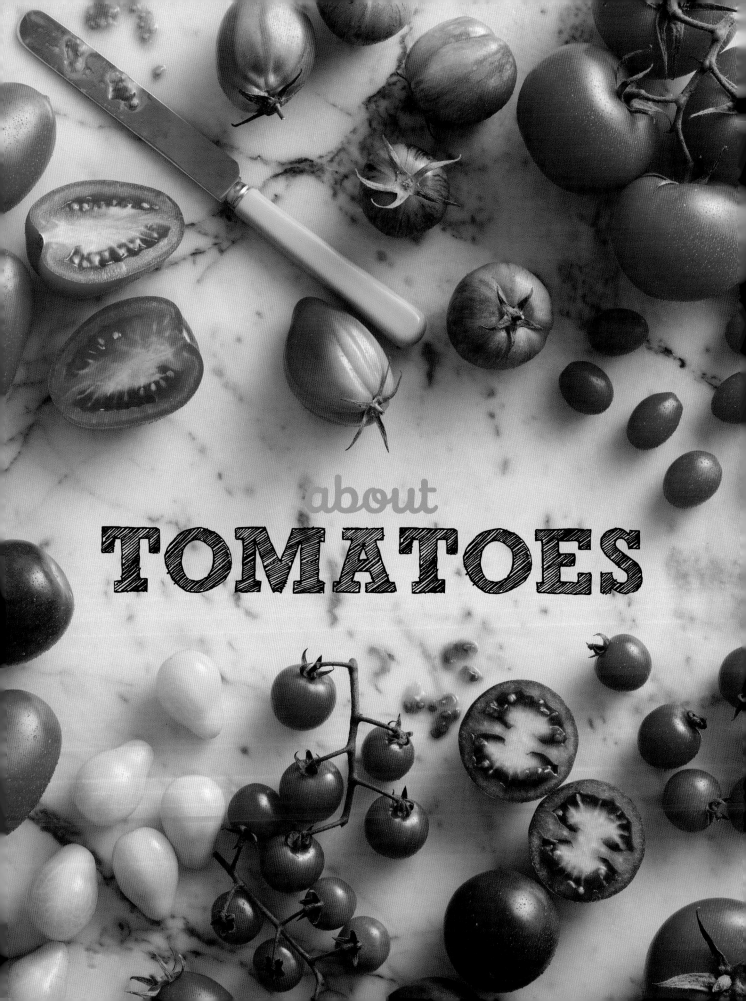

about
TOMATOES

Blanching & peeling

The easiest way to peel tomatoes is to blanch them in boiling water, which causes the skin to split.

STEP 1 Bring a large saucepan of water to the boil. Remove any green stalks from the tomatoes, then, using a sharp knife, cut a small cross in the base of each tomato.

STEP 2 Place tomatoes in boiling water for 20 seconds (you can blanch up to 3 at a time). Remove with a slotted spoon and plunge into iced water (get an adult to help you). Once the tomato has cooled, remove from the water, then peel and discard skin.

Tomatoes are very delicate and dislike the cold. If you put them in the fridge, they lose their flavour, so always store at room temperature.

Removing the seeds

STEP 1 Using the bridge technique (see Lesson #2, page 7), cut tomatoes in half. Using a spoon, scoop out and discard seeds.

STEP 2 Using the claw technique (see Lesson #2, page 7), cut tomatoes into strips, or into cubes, depending on your recipe.

Niçoise Salad

SERVES **4**
PREPARATION **20 MINS**
COOKING **20 MINS**

3 thick slices bread
60ml (¼ cup) olive oil
400g chat potatoes
250g punnet cherry
   tomatoes
200g green beans
2 spring onions
2 x 200g cans tuna in oil
40g (¼ cup) pitted
   black olives
1 baby cos lettuce

Dressing
60ml (¼ cup) olive oil
1 tbs red wine vinegar
1 tsp wholegrain mustard
1 tsp honey

MY SCORE   /10

STEP 1

Making salad dressing and croûtons

Preheat oven to 180C. Place the bread on a chopping board. Using the bridge technique (see Lesson #2, page 7), cut bread into 2cm strips, then cut into 2cm cubes. Place cubes of bread on an oven tray, then drizzle with oil. Use your hands to toss together. Bake in the oven for 6 minutes. Using oven gloves, remove tray from oven, then, using a spatula, turn the croûtons (get an adult to help). Bake for a further 6 minutes or until croûtons are golden and crisp. Set aside. To make the dressing, place the oil, vinegar, mustard and honey in a clean jar or bottle. Seal with the cap, then shake well until combined. Or whisk the ingredients together in a small bowl.

STEP 2

Preparing the vegetables

Wash the potatoes and give them a light scrub. Using the bridge technique, cut potatoes and tomatoes into quarters, then cut potato quarters in half. Place the potatoes in a small pan, cover with water, bring to the boil, then cook for 10 minutes or until just tender. Drain and leave to cool. Using scissors, top and tail (cut the ends off) the beans. Cook beans in a saucepan of simmering water for 5 minutes or until just tender. Drain in a colander in the sink (get an adult to help). Using the claw technique (see Lesson #2, page 7), thinly slice the spring onions into rounds.

STEP 3

Cooking the eggs

Place eggs in a saucepan. Run cold water into the pan until the water is 2cm above the eggs. Place pan over medium–high heat and bring to the boil. Reduce heat to a simmer and set your timer for 6 minutes. The yolks will be set but slightly gooey in the centre, but not runny. If you prefer a completely set yolk, cook for a further 3 minutes. Remove the eggs from the pan (get an adult to help you) and rinse under cold water. Once the eggs are cool, peel and cut into quarters using the bridge technique.

STEP 4

Making the salad

Using a can opener, open the tuna and drain the oil. Drain the olives. Roughly tear the lettuce, then wash the leaves and drain well. Place lettuce, beans, potatoes, tomatoes, spring onions, tuna and olives in a large salad bowl. Sprinkle with croûtons. Drizzle with dressing and gently toss everything together.

Chef's tip Add the dressing to the salad just before you are ready to eat so the croûtons don't go soggy.

PEELING EGGS

To peel cooked eggs, roll the eggs on a kitchen bench until the shells begin to crack, or tap the egg on a hard surface, rotating it until the shell cracks, then carefully peel away the shell.

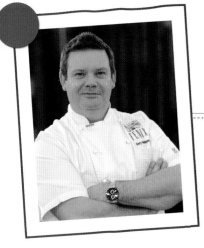

Masterclass with Gary
Chicken Schnitzel with Heirloom Tomato Salad

SERVES 2-4
PREPARATION 30 MINS
COOKING 25 MINS

2 x 200g chicken breast
  fillets
500g sourdough bread
100g (1¼ cups) grated
  parmesan
12 thyme sprigs,
  leaves picked
4 rosemary sprigs,
  leaves picked
2 tbs flat-leaf
  parsley leaves
75g (½ cup) plain flour
2 eggs
80ml (⅓ cup) milk
80ml (⅓ cup) olive oil
40g butter, chopped

Salad
4 Lebanese eggplants
80ml (⅓ cup) olive oil
½ lemon
Extra virgin olive oil,
  to drizzle
400g heirloom tomatoes*
  (such as ox heart, yellow,
  kumato and green
  zebra), cut into wedges
½ bunch basil,
  leaves picked
½ bunch flat-leaf parsley,
  leaves picked
220g cow's milk or buffalo
  mozzarella,* torn

STEP 1
Flattening the chicken
Place the chicken on a chopping board. Using a sharp knife, cut chicken in half widthwise. Place chicken between 2 sheets of plastic wrap, then, using the flat side of a meat mallet, pound to 5mm thick.

STEP 2
Making the breadcrumbs
Remove the crusts from the bread, then roughly tear the bread into pieces. Place the bread in a food processor, cover with the lid (get an adult to help), then whiz until you have fine breadcrumbs. Add herbs and season with salt and pepper, then process until finely chopped.

STEP 3
Crumbing the chicken
Place the breadcrumbs and flour in separate shallow dishes. Whisk the egg and milk together in a shallow bowl. Dust the chicken in flour, shaking off excess, then dip in egg and coat in breadcrumbs, pressing firmly to coat. Place on a plate and chill in the fridge for 20 minutes – this helps the breadcrumbs stick to the chicken.

STEP 4
Pan-frying the eggplant
To make the salad, using the bridge technique (see Lesson #2, page 7), thinly slice eggplant lengthwise. Heat oil in a frying pan over medium–high heat. Cook eggplant, in batches, for 5 minutes each side or until tender and golden. Drain on a large oven tray lined with paper towel. Squeeze over lemon, then drizzle with extra virgin oil and season to taste.

STEP 5
Making the salad
Place tomatoes, basil, parsley and mozzarella in a bowl. Drizzle with extra virgin olive oil, season, then toss to combine. Set aside.

STEP 6

Cooking the chicken

Heat oil in a large frying pan over medium heat. Cook chicken, in batches if necessary, for 3 minutes on each side or until golden. Reduce heat to low, then dot butter around chicken (get an adult to help you). Cook for a further 3 minutes, turning once, or until crisp and cooked through. Remove and drain on the paper-lined tray.

STEP 7

Serving the salad

Add eggplant to salad and toss to combine. Divide chicken among plates, then serve with the salad. * Heirloom tomatoes are from selected greengrocers and growers' markets. Buffalo mozzarella is from delis.

MY SCORE   /10

"What's great about this schnitzel is that once you've mastered the technique of flattening the chicken breasts, you can use that skill on all sorts of meat, such as veal fillets or pork steaks. Try adding different herbs to the crumb mix."

MY SCORE   /10

Isabella's Gnocchi with Tomato & Eggplant Sauce

SERVES 2-4
PREPARATION 35 MINS
COOKING 20 MINS

1 large (500g) eggplant,
   cut into 1cm cubes
60ml (¼ cup) olive oil
2 cloves garlic, crushed
2 x 400g cans chopped
   tomatoes
1 tbs caster sugar
1 tbs finely shredded basil,
   plus extra leaves,
   to serve

Ricotta gnocchi
500g fresh ricotta
150g pecorino romano
   or parmesan, grated,
   plus extra, to serve
1 egg, lightly beaten
¼ tsp ground nutmeg
300g (2 cups) plain flour

STEP 1 Season eggplant well with salt and set aside for 20 minutes (this will remove any bitterness).
STEP 2 Meanwhile, for the sauce, heat 1 tbs oil in a saucepan over medium heat. Add garlic, tomatoes and sugar, season, then bring to the boil. Reduce heat to low and simmer, stirring occasionally, for 8 minutes or until thickened. Stir in shredded basil.
STEP 3 Rinse eggplant and pat dry. Heat remaining oil in a large frying pan. Cook eggplant for 6 minutes, turning, or until golden. Drain on paper towel, then stir into tomato sauce. Set aside.
STEP 4 For the gnocchi, place ricotta, pecorino, egg, nutmeg and 35g (¼ cup) flour in a bowl. Season. Using your hands, mix to form a soft dough. Add remaining flour and mix to a stiff dough. Transfer dough to a floured surface and roll into 4 logs. Cut each roll into 8 pieces. Gently roll each ball of gnocchi over the back of a fork to create little ridges.
STEP 5 Bring a pan of water to the boil. Cook gnocchi for 2 minutes or until they rise to the surface. Remove with a slotted spoon (get an adult to help you).
STEP 6 Add drained gnocchi to the pan of sauce, then stir over low heat until warmed through. Divide among bowls, then serve with extra basil and pecorino.

ABOUT ISABELLA

Isabella, 12, from Queensland, made history when she was named the first ever *Junior MasterChef*. Inspired by her family's Sicilian heritage, this super-talented cook created impressive dishes throughout the series, including roast pheasant, spaghetti with snail sugo and this stunning ricotta gnocchi. "There are chefs who can't cook gnocchi like this," said George Calombaris. "You need to open a restaurant!"

You've done a great job of cooking the gnocchi. The flavour is great and the texture is lovely. Can I have just one more mouthful?

ANNA GARE

about
PASTA

LESSON 7
Making fresh pasta

STEP 1
Place 300g '00' flour (from supermarkets), 3 eggs, 1 tbs olive oil and a pinch of salt in a food processor. Cover with the lid, then process until mixture forms a ball. Briefly knead dough on a lightly floured surface until smooth. Shape into a disc, wrap in plastic wrap and rest at room temperature for 30 minutes.

STEP 2
Divide dough into 4 discs. Keeping remainder covered, pass 1 disc through a pasta machine on widest setting (six). Fold in half lengthwise and repeat process, without changing settings. Cut pasta if too long. Repeat process, narrowing settings 1 notch at a time, until you reach the finest setting (one). For more on fresh pasta, see the Masterclass, on page 40.

LESSON 8
Making polenta

Also known as cornmeal, polenta is made from ground dried corn and is a popular alternative to pasta in northern Italy. It can be coarse or fine, and either instant or regular.

high heat. Reduce heat to medium, then add 225g (1⅓ cups) polenta in a thin, steady stream, whisking until smooth. Whisk for 2–10 minutes (depending on type) until thickened.

STEP 1
Place 500ml milk, 500ml chicken stock and 250ml water in a large saucepan and bring to the boil over

STEP 2
Remove the pan from the heat. Season polenta and stir in 50g butter and 40g grated parmesan.

'Wet' polenta has a similar consistency to porridge and is a perfect match for rich Italian braises and hearty ragùs. Once polenta sets, it can be cut into wedges, then pan-fried, grilled or baked until golden.

Spaghetti Carbonara

SERVES **4**
PREPARATION **15 MINS**
COOKING **10 MINS**

2 eggs
2 egg yolks (see
   Lesson #20, page 91)
125ml (½ cup) pouring
   cream
40g (½ cup) finely
   grated parmesan,
   plus extra, to serve
1 tbs olive oil
250g bacon,
   cut into small strips
500g spaghetti

MY SCORE   /10

STEP 1

Preparing the egg and cream mixture

Crack the whole eggs into a large jug, add the egg yolks, cream and grated cheese. Season with freshly ground black pepper, then whisk together with a fork.

STEP 2

Cooking the bacon

Heat the olive oil in a frying pan over medium heat. Add the bacon, increase the heat to medium–high and cook for 2 minutes without stirring. Stir, then cook for 4 minutes or until the bacon is crisp. Line a plate with paper towel, then drain bacon on the plate.

STEP 3

Cooking the spaghetti

Fill a large saucepan three-quarters full with water. Bring to the boil over high heat. Add spaghetti and stir well. Cook for 8 minutes or according to packet instructions, keeping water at a good rolling boil and stirring occasionally with a long-handled spoon (get an adult to help you). Test the pasta (see Put to the Test, below). When it's cooked, drain spaghetti in a colander in the sink (get an adult to help you).

STEP 4

Combining the pasta, bacon and cream mixture

Tip spaghetti back into the warm saucepan and add bacon. Place the pan over low heat. Cook for 1 minute, stirring continuously, then add the egg mixture and immediately stir the pasta so that it's all well coated in the sauce. Keep stirring for 1 minute, then remove the pan from the heat – if you leave the pasta on the heat, the eggs will scramble. Continue stirring off the heat for 3 minutes – the heat from the saucepan and pasta will gently cook the eggs. Divide among bowls, then sprinkle with a little more parmesan to serve.

PUT TO THE TEST

Using a fork, take a piece of spaghetti from the pan, cool slightly, then taste to see if it's ready. It should be cooked but still have a little 'bite' – this is known as *al dente* in Italian.

Macaroni Cheese

SERVES 4
PREPARATION 20 MINS
COOKING 45 MINS

50g unsalted butter,
   plus extra, to grease
50g (⅓ cup) plain flour
600ml milk
200g cheddar, grated
300g macaroni pasta
2 tbs freshly grated
   parmesan

You can make one
jumbo mac cheese,
or cook it in four
smaller dishes.

MY SCORE   /10

STEP 1
Preparing the sauce
Preheat oven to 180C. Lightly grease a 2L ovenproof dish (or four 375ml (1½-cup) individual dishes). Melt butter in a small pan over low heat. Add the flour, increase heat to medium, then cook over medium heat, stirring continuously with a wooden spoon, for 1 minute until you have a smooth, glossy paste (this is called a roux). Remove from heat, add 80ml (⅓ cup) milk and stir until the mixture is smooth. Return to low heat, add a little more milk, then stir again until smooth. Continue to add milk gradually until you've added half the milk. Swap the spoon for a whisk and gradually add remaining milk, whisking continuously to prevent lumps from forming, until mixture boils and thickens. Remove from heat and stir in three-quarters of the grated cheese. Season to taste with black pepper.

STEP 2
Cooking the macaroni
Fill a large saucepan three-quarters full with cold water. Bring to the boil over high heat. Carefully add the macaroni and stir well. Cook for 8 minutes or according to packet instructions, keeping the water at a good rolling boil and stirring occasionally with a long-handled spoon (get an adult to help you).

STEP 3
Testing the macaroni
Using a fork, take a piece of macaroni from the pan, leave to cool slightly, then taste to see if it's ready. It should be cooked but still have a little 'bite' – this is known as *al dente* in Italian. When it's cooked, drain the macaroni in a colander in the sink (get an adult to help you). Shake the colander to remove any excess water.

STEP 4
Assembling the macaroni cheese
Carefully spoon macaroni into the ovenproof dish and place on an oven tray. Spoon over the cheesy sauce, then sprinkle with parmesan and remaining cheddar. Using the oven tray, lift the macaroni into the oven. Cook for 15 minutes or until the top is golden and the sauce is bubbling at the edges.

VARIATIONS
You can add all sorts of extra ingredients to your macaroni cheese. Here are a few suggestions:
* 4 bacon rashers, grilled, then chopped
* 4 ripe tomatoes, finely chopped
* 2 sausages, pan-fried, then roughly chopped
* ½ cup broccoli florets, steamed
* ½ cup frozen peas, steamed

Masterclass with George & Gary
Prawn Tortellini with Sautéed Marron and Pumpkin Purée

SERVES **4**
PREPARATION **60 MINS**
COOKING **40 MINS**

8 green marrons* (or use
   lobster or king prawns)
1 egg yolk, lightly beaten
Micro herbs,* to garnish

Pasta dough
300g (2 cups) '00' flour*
3 eggs
1 tbs olive oil

Prawn mousse
600g green prawns
1 pinch of cayenne pepper
1 egg white
125ml (½ cup) pouring
   cream
½ lemon, zested

Prawn oil
200ml olive oil
30g fennel, chopped
2 bay leaves
1 star anise
Prawn heads and shells
   (reserved from mousse)
1 tsp tomato paste

Pumpkin purée
60g butter
300g butternut pumpkin,
   peeled, coarsely grated
80ml (⅓ cup) milk

STEP 1
Making pasta dough

To make the pasta dough, place the flour, eggs, olive oil and a pinch of salt in a food processor. Place the lid on the food processor, then process until the mixture forms a ball (get an adult to help you). Remove the dough from the processor and knead briefly on a lightly floured surface until smooth. Shape into a disc, then wrap in plastic wrap and rest at room temperature for 30 minutes.

STEP 2
Making prawn mousse

Meanwhile, to make the mousse, peel and clean prawns (see Lesson #11, page 53), reserving heads and shells to make prawn oil. Place the prawn meat and cayenne in a food processor and season with salt and black pepper. Place the lid on the food processor and process until coarsely chopped (get an adult to help you). Add egg white and process until mixture is smooth. Add cream and lemon zest, and process until just combined. Don't over-process or the mixture will separate. Spoon the mousse into a bowl, taking care not to touch the blade. Cover and refrigerate until needed.

STEP 3
Making the prawn oil

To make the prawn oil, heat 1 tbs olive oil in a large frying pan over medium heat. Add the fennel, bay leaves, star anise and reserved prawn heads and shells, then cook, stirring continuously, for 3 minutes or until the shells turn bright red and fennel is tender. Stir in the tomato paste and cook, stirring, for 1 minute, then add the remaining olive oil, reduce the heat to low and cook for 20 minutes or until the oil is infused with the prawn flavour. Carefully strain the mixture through a sieve set over a bowl, then discard the solids (get an adult to help you as the oil will be very hot).

STEP 4
Preparing the marrons

Put the marrons 'to sleep' (see Chef's Tip). Fill a bowl with iced water. Bring a large saucepan of salted water to the boil. Place marrons head-first into the pan. Bring the water back to the boil and cook for 3 minutes or until marrons are a deep red colour. (It's better to undercook, rather than overcook, marron so it doesn't become tough.) Using tongs, remove marrons from pan and place in iced water (get an adult to help you). Leave to cool. Once cool, remove claws and head by twisting. Using kitchen scissors, carefully crack open marron tail and remove the meat. Using a nut cracker, carefully crack claws and remove the meat.

See next page ⟶

Chef's tip The most humane way of putting live marrons 'to sleep' is to place them in the freezer for 20 minutes before cooking.

Masterclass with George & Gary
Prawn Tortellini with Sautéed Marron and Pumpkin Purée

STEP 5
Making pumpkin purée
To make pumpkin purée, heat butter in a large frying pan over medium heat. Add pumpkin and cook, stirring, for 2 minutes or until it begins to soften. Reduce heat to low, then add milk, cover with a lid and cook, stirring occasionally, for 8 minutes or until pumpkin is soft. Cool slightly, then transfer pumpkin mixture to a food processor, cover with a lid and process until smooth (get an adult to help you). Season with salt, then spoon purée into a bowl.

STEP 6
Rolling the pasta
Divide the dough into 4 balls, then flatten each ball into a disc. Keeping the remaining dough covered, pass 1 piece through a pasta machine on the widest setting (six). Fold pasta in half lengthwise and repeat process, without changing the roller settings. Repeat process, gradually narrowing pasta machine settings 1 notch at a time, until you reach the finest setting (one), cutting pasta if it gets too long. Cover, then repeat with the remaining 3 portions.

STEP 7
Making the tortellini
Using a 10cm round cutter, cut 3 rounds from each pasta sheet to give 12 rounds in total. Brush half of each round with egg yolk, place a heaped tsp prawn mousse in the centre, then fold pasta in half to form a semi-circle, pressing the edges to seal in the filling, pushing any air out as you go. Wind the folded edge around the tip of your index finger, then press the 2 ends together to form a ring. Bring a large saucepan of salted water to the boil.

STEP 8
Finishing the dish
Cook tortellini in boiling water for 4 minutes or until pasta is tender but still has a little 'bite'. This is called *al dente*. Drain in a colander in the sink (get an adult to help you). Heat 2 tbs prawn oil in a frying pan over low–medium heat. Add marrons and cook for 2 minutes or until warmed through. Season with salt. Place a large spoonful of pumpkin purée on each plate. Divide tortellini and marrons among plates. Season, drizzle with prawn oil and scatter with herbs.
✳ Marron is from selected fishmongers. Micro herbs are from selected greengrocers and growers' markets. '00' flour is a super-fine Italian flour from delis and supermarkets; substitute plain flour.

"This is an absolutely beautiful-looking dish that delivers in loads of ways. The tortellini filling is restaurant-quality, and the prawn oil has a depth of flavour that is really hard to achieve – I love the fresh herbs, too." **MATT PRESTON**

Use lobster or prawns if you can't find marron.

MY SCORE 8/10

George and I love
this ragù – the sauce
is just so delicious.
MATT PRESTON

MY SCORE   /10

Emily's
Veal Ragù with Soft Polenta

SERVES 4
PREPARATION 20 MINS
COOKING 20 MINS

2 tbs plain flour
500g veal leg steaks,
   cut into 3cm pieces
2 tbs olive oil
20g butter
1 onion, finely chopped
2 cloves garlic,
   finely chopped
500g small Swiss brown
   mushrooms, halved
1 carrot, halved lengthwise,
   thinly sliced on an angle
1 cinnamon quill
1 star anise
500ml (2 cups) beef stock
2 tbs tomato paste
¼ cup chopped flat-leaf
   parsley leaves

Polenta

500ml (2 cups) milk
500ml (2 cups)
   salt-reduced
   chicken stock
230g (1¼ cups)
   instant polenta
40g (⅔ cup) grated
   pecorino cheese
   or parmesan
50g butter

STEP 1 Lightly dust the veal in flour, shaking off any excess. Heat 1 tbs oil and 2 tsp butter in a large, deep frying pan over medium–high heat. Add half of the veal and cook for 30 seconds each side or until sealed. Remove from the pan and set aside. Repeat with the remaining oil, butter and veal. Set aside.

STEP 2 Add the onion to the pan and cook, stirring, for 2 minutes over medium heat or until softened. Add the garlic and mushrooms and cook, stirring, for 2 minutes or until mushrooms are slightly softened. Add carrot, cinnamon, star anise, stock and tomato paste, and stir until combined. Return veal to the pan, bring to the boil, then reduce the heat to low and simmer for 10 minutes or until sauce is reduced and veal is tender. Stir in the parsley.

STEP 3 Meanwhile, to make the polenta, place the milk, stock and 250ml (1 cup) water in a large saucepan and bring to the boil over high heat. Reduce the heat to medium, then add the polenta in a thin, steady stream, whisking continuously, until smooth. Continue to whisk for 2 minutes or until thickened. Stir in the cheese and butter, then season to taste. Divide the polenta among bowls, then top with the ragù and serve.

ABOUT EMILY

Emily is 11 years old and comes from South Australia. In the butcher challenge in Heat Five of the Top 50, Emily created a standout dish of rabbit and mushroom ragù on creamy, soft polenta. Rabbit can be a bit tricky to come across, but never fear, because Emily's recipe also works a treat with veal.

about
RICE

LESSON 9
Go with the grain

* Long-grain rice is one of the most common types of rice as it's quick and easy to cook. Serve it with stir-fries. Use leftover long-grain to make fried rice.
* Basmati rice grows mainly in the foothills of the Himalayas in India and Pakistan. It has a lovely flavour and is great with curries or in biryani, a spiced rice dish.
* Brown rice has a layer of fibre (called bran) on the surface of the grain, making it a healthier alternative to regular white rice (which has had the husk removed). Its nutty flavour and chewy texture work well in salads.
* Arborio, carnaroli and vialone nano are short-grained rices, which give risotto a beautiful creamy texture.

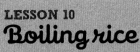

One cup of raw rice will give you two cups of cooked rice. Once the rice is cooked, fluff up with a fork to separate the grains and break up any lumps.

LESSON 10
Boiling rice

STEP 1
Place 200g (1 cup) rice in a sieve and rinse under running water until water runs clear. Place rice in a saucepan filled with 8 cups (2L) salted water. Bring to the boil, stirring, then reduce heat to medium and cook for 12–14 minutes. Test rice after 10 minutes – it should be tender but firm in the centre.

STEP 2
Drain the rice into a colander in the sink (get an adult to help you). Rinse briefly under hot water to separate grains before draining well again. Run a fork through the rice to separate the grains. This prevents the rice setting into a solid mass.

Oven-baked Pea Risotto

SERVES 6
PREPARATION 20 MINS
COOKING 30 MINS

350g fresh peas (taken
  from 1kg peas in the pod,
  or use frozen peas)
2 cloves garlic
3 spring onions
1 tbs olive oil
1 tbs butter
1 tsp chopped thyme
  leaves
385g (1¾ cups) arborio rice
1.25L (5 cups) chicken
  stock
50g (⅔ cup) finely grated
  parmesan, plus shaved
  parmesan, to serve

STEP 1
Preparing the vegetables
Preheat oven to 180C.
Cook the peas in a
saucepan of boiling water
for 2 minutes or until
tender, then drain in a
colander in the sink (get
an adult to help). Divide
peas between 2 bowls.
Mash 1 bowl of peas using
a potato masher. Peel and
crush the garlic. Using the
claw technique (see Lesson
2, page 7), thinly slice
the spring onion.c

STEP 2
Preparing the risotto
Heat the oil and butter in
a heavy-based saucepan
over low–medium heat.
Add the spring onions and
cook, stirring, for 5 minutes
or until soft. Add the garlic
and thyme, and cook,
stirring, for 1 minute. Add
rice and cook, stirring, for
2 minutes until well coated.
This is called 'toasting'
the rice – it ensures every
rice grain warms up and
cooks evenly.

STEP 3
Baking the risotto
Place stock in a saucepan
and bring to the boil
over high heat. Spoon
the rice mixture into a
3L ovenproof dish. Very
carefully add the hot stock
and stir to combine (get an
adult to help you). Place
the dish in the oven and
cook for 30 minutes or
until the liquid is absorbed
and rice is tender. Using
oven gloves, take the dish
out of the oven (get an
adult to help you), stir in
parmesan and mashed and
whole peas, then return
dish to oven for a further
5 minutes or until rice is
cooked but still has a little
bite (this is called 'al dente'
in Italian). Divide risotto
among bowls and serve
with shaved parmesan.

GO GREEN
Did you know that just one serving
of peas contains as much vitamin C
as two apples and more fibre than
a slice of bread? For an instant
health hit and a burst of flavour,
add a handful of peas to your
favourite soups, salads and pastas.

Risotto means 'little rice'

MY SCORE /10

Masterclass with Anna
Chicken, Chorizo & Prawn Paella

SERVES 4
PREPARATION 20 MINS
COOKING 20 MINS

1 chorizo sausage
250g chicken thigh fillets
1 tsp smoked Spanish
   paprika
1 onion
1 small red capsicum,
   cut into 1cm pieces
100g green beans,
   cut into 3cm lengths
1 long red chilli
750ml (3 cups) chicken
   stock
1 tsp saffron threads
60ml (¼ cup) olive oil
8 medium green king
   prawns, peeled, cleaned
   (see Lesson #11, page 53)
2 cloves garlic
6 sprigs thyme
200g (1 cup) Calasparra
   (paella rice)*
   or arborio rice
8 black mussels, scrubbed,
   bearded (see Lesson #12,
   page 53)
Flat-leaf parsley sprigs and
   lemon wedges, to serve

STEP 1
Preparing ingredients
Using the claw technique (see Lesson #2, page 7), cut chorizo into 1cm-thick slices on the diagonal, then place in a bowl. Using the same technique, cut chicken into 3cm pieces and place in a second bowl with paprika, then toss well to coat. Cut the onion and capsicum into 1cm squares, using both the claw and bridge techniques, cut the beans into 3cm lengths. Using the bridge technique, cut chilli in half lengthwise, then, using the claw technique, cut into strips and finely chop. Make sure not to rub your eyes when cutting the chilli and wash your hands immediately to avoid stinging.

STEP 2
Pan-frying the meat
Combine chicken stock and saffron in a large saucepan over high heat and bring to the boil. Transfer to a jug (get an adult to help you), then cover with foil to keep warm. Heat 2 tbs olive oil in a 24cm frying or paella pan over medium–high heat. Add the chorizo and chicken, and cook, turning the pieces over, for 3 minutes or until lightly browned. Add the prawns and stir to coat in oil, then transfer everything to a plate. Reserve the pan.

STEP 3
Cooking the onion
Heat remaining 1 tbs olive oil in the reserved pan over medium heat. Add chopped onion and chilli. Using a garlic crusher, crush garlic into the pan, then pull leaves off thyme sprigs and place in the pan. Stir mixture for 5 minutes or until onions are soft.

STEP 4
Toasting the rice
Add the rice and stir for 1 minute or until the rice is glazed with oil. This is called 'toasting the rice', but you don't want it to get any colour like toast. Using the spoon, spread out the rice evenly to cover the base of the pan.

STEP 5
Adding the vegetables
Top rice with chicken, chorizo and prawns, then scatter with beans and capsicum. Gently pour stock into pan, then simmer for 10 minutes without stirring. The rice will absorb some of the liquid.

STEP 6
Adding the mussels
Place mussels on their side over the rice, then cook for a further 10 minutes or until they open. All stock should be absorbed and the rice *al dente* (firm to the bite). Season. Scatter with parsley sprigs, then spoon paella among bowls. Serve with lemon wedges.
✱ Calasparra is a special short-grained Spanish rice used for paella. You can buy it at delis and specialist food stores; substitute arborio.

MY SCORE /10

The trick to a good paella is making sure all the ingredients are cooked in time with the rice. Start by sealing off all your meats and vegies in the same pan you cook the paella in so all the flavours are captured.

about
SEAFOOD

LESSON 11
Peeling & cleaning prawns

Remove the smell of prawns from your fingers by rubbing your hands with the cut side of a lemon before washing with warm, soapy water.

STEP 1
To peel a prawn, twist off and discard the head, then remove the legs. Peel the shell from the prawn. If you also want to remove the tail, squeeze the tail and twist it off the body.

STEP 2
To clean a prawn, using a small sharp knife, make a slit along the back of the prawn to expose the dark 'vein'. Pull out and discard the vein. To clean a prawn without cutting the back, use your fingers to gently pull the vein through the opening at the head end.

LESSON 12
Preparing mussels

STEP 1 Rinse mussels under cold running water. Using a clean scourer or brush, scrub the shells to remove any barnacles and sand.
STEP 2 To remove the furry beard, hold the mussel firmly in one hand while pulling on the beard with the other – it should break free of the mussel. Discard any mussels that don't close when tapped sharply on the bench.

Marinated Prawns

SERVES 4
PREPARATION 15 MINS
COOKING 10 MINS

1kg medium green prawns
1 lemon
2 cloves garlic, crushed
1 tsp sesame oil
1 tbs olive oil
60ml (¼ cup) soy sauce
⅓ cup coriander leaves,
   finely chopped
Steamed rice (see Lesson
   #10, page 47), broccolini
   and snow peas, to serve

STEP 1
Peeling the prawns
Prepare the prawns
(see Lesson #11, page 53),
then place the peeled
prawns in a bowl.

STEP 2
Making the marinade
Using the bridge technique
(see Lesson #2, page 7),
cut the lemon in half. Place
1 lemon half, flesh-side
down, over a juicer. Press
down firmly, then twist to
release juice. Repeat with
remaining half. Combine
lemon juice, garlic, sesame
oil, olive oil, soy sauce and
coriander in a small bowl.

STEP 3
Baking the prawns
Place the prawns in a glass
or ceramic dish. Pour the
marinade over the prawns
and toss to coat. Cover and
refrigerate for 30 minutes.
Preheat oven to 180C.
Remove prawns from the
marinade and place in an
ovenproof dish. Cover with
foil and cook in the oven for
10 minutes or until pink and
cooked through. Serve with
rice and vegetables.

We love this tangy lemon marinade with chicken, and the spicy one's great with beef.

Lemon & herb marinade
Juice of 1 lemon
60ml (¼ cup) olive oil
2 cloves garlic, crushed
⅓ cup flat-leaf
   parsley leaves,
   finely chopped

Spicy marinade
1 tsp ground coriander
1 tsp ground cumin
1 tsp paprika
1 tbs honey
¼ cup mint leaves,
   finely chopped
60ml (¼ cup) olive oil

MY SCORE /10

Lemon Fish Fingers

SERVES **4**
PREPARATION **20 MINS**
COOKING **20 MINS**

Sunflower oil, to grease
500g skinless firm white
   fish fillets (such as ling)
4 slices bread
½ lemon
75g (½ cup) plain flour
1 egg
120g (1 cup) frozen peas
Mayonnaise, lemon wedges
   and potato wedges (see
   recipe, page 58), to
   serve

These fish fingers
are also fantastic
made with salmon
or ocean trout.
To make an easy
tartare sauce,
stir some lemon
zest, capers and
parsley into your
mayonnaise.

MY SCORE **/10**

STEP 1
Pin-boning the fish
Preheat oven to 190C. Brush a little oil over an oven tray. Place the fish fillet on a chopping board. Run your fingers over the fish to check for bones. If you find any bones, pull them out with a pair of tweezers – this is called pin-boning.

STEP 2
Slicing the fish
Using the claw technique (see Lesson #2, page 7), cut fish into 1cm strips.

STEP 3
Making breadcrumbs
Remove the crusts from the bread, then roughly tear the bread into pieces. Place the bread in a food processor, cover with the lid (get an adult to help), then whiz until you have fine breadcrumbs.

STEP 4
Crumbing the fish
Using a box grater, hold the top of the grater firmly with one hand. With your other hand, hold the lemon at the top end of the grater and push down the side of the grater with the smallest holes – try to avoid grating the bitter white pith. Using a pastry brush, remove zest from grater, then combine with breadcrumbs on a plate. Place flour on a separate plate and season with pepper. Crack egg into a shallow bowl, add 1 tbs water and beat with a fork. Dust fish pieces with flour, shake off excess, then dip in egg and coat in breadcrumbs. Place on a plate and chill in the fridge for 20 minutes – this helps the crumbs stick to the fish.

STEP 5
Cooking the fish and the peas
Place the fish on the greased oven tray and bake for 5 minutes. Using oven gloves, carefully remove the tray from the oven, then, using a spatula, carefully turn the fish over (get an adult to help you). Cook in the oven for a further 5 minutes until the fish is golden on the outside and cooked through in the middle. Meanwhile, cook the peas in a saucepan of boiling water for 2 minutes or until tender, then drain in a colander in the sink (get an adult to help). Serve the fish fingers with peas, mayonnaise, lemon and potato wedges. **See next page.** →

Potato Wedges

SERVES **4**
PREPARATION **10 MINS**
COOKING **35 MINS**

**600g red-skinned
potatoes (such as
desiree), washed
2 tbs sunflower oil**

STEP 1
Cutting the potatoes
Preheat oven to 190C.
Using the bridge technique
(see Lesson #2, page 7),
cut potatoes in half, then
cut each potato half into
4 wedges. Place the potato
wedges in a bowl, drizzle
with the sunflower oil, then
use your hands to toss until
the wedges are coated.

STEP 2
Coating in oil
Alternatively, place potato
wedges in a plastic bag,
add the oil, then scrunch
the potatoes around in the
bag until they are coated
in the oil. This method is
handy if you want to add
extra flavourings (see
Spice It Up).

STEP 3
Baking the wedges
Spread potato wedges
onto an oven tray and roast
for 15 minutes. Using oven
gloves, carefully remove
the tray from the oven,
then, using a spatula, turn
wedges over (get an adult
to help you). Return the
tray to the oven and cook
for a further 20 minutes
or until the wedges are
tender and golden.

*Orange sweet
potato (kumara)
wedges also
work a treat!*

Spice it up
Add extra flavour to your
wedges with a pinch of
paprika, some freshly
ground black pepper or
a sprinkle of garlic salt.

Salmon Fishcakes

SERVES **8**
PREPARATION **25 MINS**
COOKING **30 MINS**

450g desiree potatoes,
   peeled
2 x 200g salmon fillets
500ml (2 cups) milk
3 lemon slices
3 bay leaves
8 black peppercorns
⅓ cup flat-leaf parsley,
   finely chopped
50g (⅓ cup) plain flour
2 eggs
100g fresh breadcrumbs
   (see Step 3, page 57)
Sunflower oil, to grease
Lemon wedges and
   green salad, to serve

STEP 1
Mashing the potatoes
Place the potatoes in a saucepan of cold water, bring to the boil over high heat, then cook for 30 minutes or until just tender. Drain in a colander in the sink (get an adult to help). Return to pan and mash until smooth. Set aside.

STEP 2
Preparing the salmon
Run your fingers over the salmon to check for bones. If you find any, pull them out with tweezers. Place salmon in a wide saucepan or frying pan. Pour milk over salmon to cover, then add bay leaves, lemon and peppercorns.

STEP 3
Poaching the salmon
Place the frying pan over medium heat and bring to a gentle simmer. As soon as the liquid bubbles, turn the heat down to low, then poach the salmon for 7 minutes. Remove the pan from the heat. **See next page.** ⟶

Did you know?
Poaching is a gentle cooking method where food is simmered in a liquid, such as milk, water or stock, until it's tender.

Salmon Fishcakes

STEP 4

Cooling the salmon

Using a spatula, lift the salmon fillets out of the poaching liquid, then transfer the salmon to a plate and cool.

STEP 5

Breaking up the salmon

Using your hands, peel and discard skin. Break salmon into pieces, then flake into small chunks. Remove and discard any bones.

STEP 6

Combining ingredients

Place mashed potatoes, salmon and parsley in a bowl, then season with pepper. Using a spoon, stir everything together until combined.

STEP 7

Shaping the fishcakes

Using your hands, place the salmon mixture on a chopping board and shape into a long rectangle. Cut the log into quarters, then cut each piece in half to make 8 pieces in total. Roll each piece into a ball, then flatten slightly to make 8 discs.

STEP 8

Crumbing the fishcakes

Place the flour and breadcrumbs on separate plates. Crack eggs into a shallow bowl, add 1 tbs water and beat with a fork. Dust fishcakes with flour, shake off excess, then dip in egg and coat in breadcrumbs. Place on a plate and chill in the fridge for 20 minutes – this helps the crumbs stick to the fishcakes. Preheat oven to 200C. Lightly grease an oven tray. Place fishcakes on the tray and bake for 10 minutes. Using oven gloves, remove tray from oven, then, using a spatula, turn the fishcakes (get an adult to help you). Return tray to oven for a further 10 minutes or until light golden. Serve with lemon wedges and salad.

SMART STUFF

Try to eat at least two serves of fish each week, including one serve of oily fish, such as salmon or trout. Salmon is called a 'smart food', because its high levels of protein, vitamins and omega 3s are great for your brain.

MY SCORE   /10

What I love is the salmon – to cook salmon like that when you're not a professional is really hard to do.

GARY MEHIGAN

MY SCORE   /10

Cassidy's
Salmon with Dukkah, Tomato Chutney and Star Anise Cream

SERVES 4
PREPARATION 25 MINS
COOKING 25 MINS

45g (⅓ cup) dukkah*
4 x 150g skinless salmon
   fillets, pin-boned
   (see Step 1, page 57)
60ml (¼ cup) olive oil
1 leek, white part only,
   quartered lengthwise,
   sliced
1 carrot, cut into
   1cm pieces
2 stalks celery,
   cut into 1cm pieces
4 vine leaves in brine*

Tomato chutney

4 vine-ripened tomatoes,
   seeds removed,
   chopped (see Lesson
   #6, page 27)
2 small pickling onions,
   finely chopped
2 tbs brown sugar
1 tbs tarragon vinegar*
1 cinnamon quill
4 cloves

Star anise cream

2 star anise
250ml (1 cup) pouring
   cream
1 tbs lemon juice
1 sprig rosemary
2 tsp plain flour

STEP 1 Dust top of salmon fillets with dukkah. Cover and place in the fridge.
STEP 2 To make chutney, place tomatoes, onion, sugar, vinegar, cinnamon, cloves, 125ml (½ cup) water and ½ tsp salt in a saucepan over medium–high heat. Bring to the boil, then reduce heat to medium and simmer, stirring occasionally, for 20 minutes or until thickened.
STEP 3 Meanwhile, heat oil in a large frying pan over medium heat. Add leek, carrot and celery, and cook, stirring, for 5 minutes or until tender.
STEP 4 To make the star anise cream, place star anise and 100ml water in a saucepan over high heat and boil for 5 minutes (this will infuse the water). Remove star anise (get an adult to help you), then add cream, lemon juice, rosemary and flour to the infused water. Whisk continuously over medium–high heat for 2 minutes or until mixture boils and thickens. Remove from the heat.
STEP 5 Half-fill a wok or large saucepan with water and bring to the boil over high heat. Line a bamboo steamer basket with baking paper, then top with vine leaves and salmon fillets. Cover, then steam over the pan of boiling water for 4 minutes or until salmon is just cooked through.
STEP 6 To serve, using a spatula, transfer salmon to a tray. Tear vine leaves into pieces, then stir through vegetables. Divide vegetables among plates and top with salmon, then drizzle with star anise cream and serve with tomato chutney.
✻ Dukkah and tarragon vinegar are from delis and specialist food stores. Vine leaves are from supermarkets.

ABOUT CASSIDY

Cassidy is 12 years old and lives in Victoria. In the Hot and Cold Challenge in Episode Eight, Cassidy avoided elimination with this creative steamed salmon dish and a mille-feuille with strawberry coulis. Anna Gare said, "the salmon is soft and succulent, and I love the dukkah flavours."

I'm flabbergasted that a junior cook can make a dish like this!

GEORGE CALOMBARIS

MY SCORE /10

Alex's
Seafood soup

SERVES 4
PREPARATION 25 MINS
COOKING 10 MINS

20 green prawns
1 tbs extra virgin olive oil
50g butter
4 cloves garlic,
    finely chopped
500ml (2 cups) fish stock
250ml (1 cup) tomato
    pasta sauce
25 black mussels,
    cleaned (see Lesson #12,
    page 53)
2 x 250g skinless gemfish
    fillets, bones removed,
    cut into 2cm pieces
¼ cup chopped flat-leaf
    parsley leaves
Lemon wedges and crusty
    baguette (optional),
    to serve

STEP 1 Peel and clean the prawns (see Lesson #11, page 53), leaving tails intact and reserving the heads. Using a sharp knife, butterfly the prawns by slicing along the underside, from head-end to tail, without cutting all the way through.
STEP 2 Heat the oil and butter in a large saucepan over medium–high heat. Add the garlic and reserved prawn heads, and cook, stirring, for 1 minute. Add stock and 250ml (1 cup) water, and bring to the boil.
STEP 3 Once the stock comes to the boil, remove pan from heat and strain liquid through a colander into a bowl (get an adult to help you). Discard prawn heads. Return the stock to the pan. Add pasta sauce and mussels, and stir to combine. Cover and bring to the boil over high heat. Cook for 1 minute or until shells open.
STEP 4 Add the prawns and fish, and cook a further 2 minutes or until the seafood is cooked through. Stir in the parsley, then season with salt and pepper. Serve with lemon and crusty bread.

ABOUT ALEX

Eleven-year-old Alex, from New South Wales, wowed the judges in Heat Three of the Top 50 when he presented his *goût de la mer*, which means 'taste of the sea' in French. Matt Preston said this delicious soup, loaded with prawns, mussels and fish, is "a perfectly balanced dish and a really smart bit of cooking".

about
MEAT

LESSON 13
Cooking & testing meat

STEP 1
Heat a frying pan over medium–high het before adding the steak (this seals the surface, trapping in juices). Instead of oiling the pan, brush the steak with olive oil to prevent it sticking. Once you've added the steak to the pan, only turn it once. If you turn the steak too often, it will dry out. Always use tongs to handle steak, as they won't pierce the meat and allow juices to escape.

STEP 2
Cook a 2cm-thick piece of steak for 2 minutes on each side for rare, 4 minutes for medium and 6 minutes for well done. To test if your steak is done, press the centre with the back of the tongs. The steak will feel soft it it's rare, slightly firmer and springy when it's medium and very firm when it's well done. Transfer steak to a plate, cover loosely with foil and set aside for 5–10 minutes to rest. This allows the juices to settle and the muscle fibres to relax, ensuring the steak is tender.

Tying a beef fillet ensures it maintains its shape and cooks through perfectly.

LESSON 14
Preparing a whole fillet

To prepare a whole fillet of beef for roasting, using a simple knot, tie kitchen string around the meat at 3cm intervals, then wrap the string once around the length of the meat. This ensures the meat doesn't lose its shape during cooking. Rub the fillet with olive oil and season with salt and pepper just before cooking.

Beef Burgers with Sweet Potato Chips

SERVES 6
PREPARATION 15 MINS
COOKING 20 MINS

2 spring onions, trimmed
2 tbs olive oil,
   plus extra to brush
1 small clove garlic,
   crushed
500g beef mince
⅓ cup flat-leaf parsley
   leaves, finely chopped
1 egg, beaten
1 orange sweet potato
   (kumara)
6 hamburger buns, halved
6 iceberg lettuce leaves
3 tomatoes, sliced
6 slices canned beetroot,
   drained
6 slices cheddar
¼ cup tomato sauce

STEP 1
Cooking the vegies
Using the bridge technique (see Lesson #2, page 7), halve the spring onions lengthwise, then cut into small pieces. Heat 1 tbs oil in a frying pan over low heat. Add onions and garlic, and cook, stirring occasionally, for 5 minutes or until soft. Cool, then place in a large bowl with the beef and parsley. Add egg and, using your hands, mix everything together.

STEP 2
Shaping the patties
Shape into 6 patties. Place on a tray, then cover with plastic wrap and refrigerate for 30 minutes to firm up. Preheat oven to 190C. Brush an oven tray with a little oil and place the burger patties on it. Bake in the oven for 10 minutes, then, using oven gloves, remove the tray from the oven (get an adult to help you). Using a spatula, turn the patties over, then bake for a further 10 minutes or until cooked through.

STEP 3
Making the chips
Meanwhile, peel the sweet potato. Using the bridge technique, cut into 1cm slices, then into 1cm chips. Place in a bowl with remaining oil and toss to coat. Spread chips in a single layer on an oven tray. Bake for 15 minutes or until crisp on one side. Using oven gloves, remove the tray from the oven (get an adult to help you), then, using a spatula, turn the chips. Bake for a further 15 minutes or until golden and cooked through.

STEP 4
Making the burgers
Toast the burger buns, then fill with lettuce, tomato, beetroot, a beef pattie, cheese and tomato sauce. Serve with the chips.

Sweet potatoes make awesome chips – crunchy on the outside and fluffy within!

MY SCORE   /10

Chicken & Corn Burgers

SERVES 6
PREPARATION 20 MINS
COOKING 20 MINS

8 slices brown bread
120g cheddar
2 spring onions
500g chicken mince
125g can corn kernels,
 rinsed, drained
75g (½ cup) plain flour
1 egg, lightly beaten
1 tbs milk
Olive oil, to brush
6 hamburger buns, halved
½ cup mayonnaise
6 lettuce leaves
1 avocado, sliced
1 Lebanese cucumber,
 thinly sliced
1 carrot, thinly sliced

STEP 1
Making the breadcrumbs
Remove the crusts from
the bread, then roughly
tear the bread into pieces.
Place the bread in a food
processor, cover with the
lid (get an adult to help),
then whiz until you have
fine breadcrumbs.

STEP 2
Making the patties
Using a box grater, grate
the cheese. Place in a bowl.
Using the bridge technique
(Lesson #2, page 7), halve
spring onions lengthwise,
then cut into small pieces
and place in bowl with
cheese. Add chicken, corn
and 1 cup crumbs. Using
your hands, mix together
until combined. Shape into
6 patties. Place on a tray,
then cover and refrigerate
for 30 minutes until firm.

STEP 3
Shaping and cooking
the patties
Preheat oven to 190C.
Place flour and remaining
breadcrumbs in separate
shallow bowls. Combine
beaten egg and milk in
another bowl. Dust patties
in flour, shaking off excess.
Dip in egg, then coat with
breadcrumbs. Place patties
on a lightly oiled oven tray.
Bake in the oven for
10 minutes, then, using
oven gloves, remove tray
from oven (get an adult to
help you). Using a spatula,
turn patties, then bake
for a further 10 minutes
or until cooked through.
Toast burger buns, then fill
with mayonnaise, lettuce,
a burger pattie, avocado,
cucumber and carrot.

TOP BUN
Add extra flavour and
nutrition to your burgers
by choosing a wholemeal,
multigrain or seeded
bun. There are plenty of
delicious combinations
to choose from.

Lamb & thyme burger

Use the technique for the chicken burger (pictured below) to create a delicious lamb version. Using a pair of scissors, cut ½ cup dried apricots into pieces, snip 2 tbs thyme leaves, then place in a bowl with 500g lamb mince. Add 1 beaten egg, season, then use your hands to mix together. Shape into 6 patties. Place on a tray, then cover and chill for 30 minutes. Preheat oven to 190C and grill to high. Brush an oven tray with oil. Place patties on tray and bake for 10 minutes. Using oven gloves, remove tray from oven, then use a spatula to turn patties (get an adult to help). Return to oven for a further 10 minutes until cooked through. Split 6 burger buns and grill for 1 minute or until toasted. Fill buns with lettuce, tomato, beetroot, lamb patties and barbecue sauce. Makes 6.

MY SCORE   /10

Masterclass with George
Beef Fillet with Garlic Butter and Tomato Concassé

SERVES 4
PREPARATION 35 MINS
COOKING 20 MINS

Concassé is a French term used to describe chopped or diced vegetables. Tomato concassé makes a lovely, simple garnish for steak.

1 bulb garlic
60ml (¼ cup) olive oil, plus extra, to drizzle
200g butter, softened, chopped
¼ cup flat-leaf parsley leaves
1 tsp rosemary leaves
2 tsp fresh oregano
1 tbs Dijon mustard
8 large tomatoes
4 x 180g beef eye-fillet steaks
Baby rocket leaves, to serve
Balsamic vinegar, to drizzle

STEP 1
Roasting the garlic
Preheat oven to 180C. Pull garlic bulb apart to separate the cloves, then place cloves on a sheet of foil and drizzle with a little olive oil. Wrap up the foil to enclose the garlic. Roast in the oven for 15 minutes or until tender. Using oven gloves, remove the garlic from the oven (get an adult to help you). Open the parcel and cool.

Chef's tip Roasting garlic softens the flavour and adds a hint of sweetness.

STEP 2
Making garlic butter
Squeeze 4 roasted garlic cloves out of the skins and into a food processor. Add butter, parsley, rosemary, oregano and mustard to the processor, season, then cover with the lid (get an adult to help you). Process until herbs are finely chopped and butter mixture is well combined. Place a sheet of plastic wrap on the bench. Spread butter in a 10cm line down the centre of the plastic, then roll up to enclose and form a log, twisting ends to seal so it resembles a bonbon. Freeze for 30 minutes or until firm.

STEP 3
Making tomato concassé
Meanwhile, to make tomato concassé, blanch and peel the tomatoes (see Lesson #5, page 27), then remove the seeds (see Lesson #6, page 27). Pat tomatoes dry with paper towel. Using the bridge and claw techniques (see Lesson #2, page 7), cut the tomato quarters into 8mm cubes. Place in a bowl with 2 tbs oil and season with salt and pepper.

STEP 4
Cooking the beef
Using kitchen string, truss the beef (tie around the centre) so it retains its shape during cooking. Season beef with salt and pepper. Heat remaining 1 tbs oil in a large frying pan over medium–high heat. Cook steaks for 3 minutes on each side for medium–rare or until cooked to your liking. Transfer beef to a plate, cover loosely with foil, then rest for 3 minutes. Remove kitchen string. Place some rocket on 4 plates, then top with steaks. Remove plastic from garlic butter and slice off 4 x 1cm-thick rounds. Top each steak with a round of butter. Spoon tomato concassé onto the plate, scatter with remaining roasted garlic, then drizzle with balsamic.

MY SCORE /10

HIGH STEAKS
✳ Always bring your steaks to room temperature before cooking, as this will prevent the meat from becoming tough.
✳ Using paper towel, pat steaks dry before cooking, so the meat caramelises nicely.
✳ For juicy, tender steaks, rest for 3–5 minutes before serving.

Masterclass with Stephanie
Leg of Lamb with Herb Crust & Roasted Vegetables

SERVES 4
PREPARATION 40 MINS
COOKING 1 HOUR

1.5kg butterflied leg
   of lamb
2 tbs Dijon mustard
2 tomatoes, halved,
   seeded (see Lesson #6,
   page 27)
40g butter
1 baby cos, shredded
250g fresh peas in the
   pod, podded
250ml (1 cup) veal stock
60ml (¼ cup) verjuice*

Roast vegetables
4 eschalots, peeled, boiled
   for 5 minutes to soften
4 sebago potatoes,
   peeled, quartered
2 parsnips, peeled,
   chopped
2 carrots, peeled, chopped
200g butternut pumpkin,
   peeled, chopped
4 cloves garlic
2 tbs olive oil
2 bay leaves
2 sprigs thyme

Herb crust
105g (1½ cups) packaged
   breadcrumbs
1 lemon, zested
1 tbs chopped rosemary
1 tbs thyme leaves
1 clove garlic,
   finely chopped
80g butter, melted

STEP 1
Roasting the vegetables
Preheat oven to 200C. For the roast vegetables, toss all ingredients together in a large roasting pan. Season with salt and pepper, then roast for 20 minutes.

STEP 2
Making the herb crust
Meanwhile, to make the herb crust, combine the breadcrumbs, zest, herbs, garlic and melted butter in a bowl, then season. Place lamb on a chopping board and trim off excess fat. Turn over and season well. Turn fat-side up, then brush with mustard and top with two-thirds crust mixture, pressing down with your fingertips.

STEP 3
Roasting lamb and tomatoes
Place tomatoes in a small ovenproof dish, then fill with the remaining crust mixture. After the vegetables have roasted for 20 minutes, using oven gloves, remove pan from oven (get an adult to help) and place lamb on an oven rack placed over vegetables, then place on top shelf of oven. Place tomatoes on lower shelf. Roast for 30 minutes or until lamb is medium–rare or cooked to your liking and tomatoes are tender. Set aside for 15 minutes.

STEP 4
Cooking peas
Meanwhile, melt the butter in a small saucepan over low heat. Add the lettuce and cook, stirring occasionally, for 2 minutes or until wilted. Add the peas and 125ml (½ cup) water, cover and cook for 8 minutes or until the peas are tender. Drain, then place the peas in a bowl. Keep warm.

STEP 5
Deglazing the pan
To make the sauce, remove lamb and vegetables from the pan, leaving liquid and garlic in the pan. Place pan over medium heat. Add stock and verjuice, and stir (this is known as deglazing) for 2 minutes or until combined. Squash garlic cloves with the back of a spoon, then strain sauce into a small pan. Simmer over high heat for 5 minutes or until reduced slightly. Pour into a jug.

STEP 6
Serving the roast
Slice meat, then serve with roast vegetables, tomatoes, peas and the sauce.
✳ Verjuice is the juice of unripe, usually green, grapes; it's found in delis and selected supermarkets. Substitute dry white wine.

MY SCORE   /10

This tastes absolutely perfect! I can almost see 'Pierre's Pies' up in lights.
ANNA GARE

MY SCORE /10

Pierre's
Lamb Wellingtons with Mushroom & Spinach Duxelles

SERVES 4
PREPARATION 30 MINS
COOKING 25 MINS

2 tbs olive oil
2 x 200g lamb backstraps
40g butter
16 small button
  mushrooms, thinly sliced
200g baby spinach
3 sheets frozen puff pastry,
  thawed in the fridge
2 tsp Dijon mustard
1 egg, lightly beaten
2 desiree potatoes,
  peeled, finely chopped
1 small orange sweet
  potato (kumara),
  peeled, finely chopped
2 cloves garlic, thinly sliced
1 large onion, halved,
  thinly sliced
60ml (¼ cup) olive oil
70g (½ cup) pine nuts,
  roasted
2 tsp finely chopped
  thyme leaves

STEP 1 Preheat oven to 220C. Heat oil in a large frying pan over medium–high heat. Add lamb and cook for 1 minute each side or until browned. Remove and set aside.
STEP 2 Melt butter in the frying pan over medium–high heat, add mushrooms and cook, stirring occasionally, for 2 minutes or until softened. Add half the spinach and cook a further 1 minute or until wilted. Set the mushroom duxelles aside to cool.
STEP 3 Place a sheet of puff pastry on a piece of baking paper. Place a piece of lamb in the centre of the pastry sheet and spread with 1 tsp Dijon mustard. Spoon half the mushroom duxelles over the lamb. Fold pastry over lamb and roll up like a parcel, turning seam-side down. Trim ends and seal with a fork. Lightly brush with egg. Repeat to make another Wellington. Cut remaining sheet of pastry into 2cm strips. Place over Wellingtons in a lattice pattern, pressing edges to seal. Lightly brush with egg. Place on an oven tray, then bake for 20 minutes or until golden.
STEP 4 Meanwhile, heat oil in a large, deep frying pan over medium–high heat. Add potatoes, sweet potato, garlic and onion. Season, then cook, stirring occasionally, for 10 minutes or until tender. Add the remaining spinach and cook, stirring, for 1 minute or until wilted, then stir in pine nuts and thyme. Season to taste. Cut the Wellingtons in half, then divide among plates and serve with vegetables.

ABOUT PIERRE
Pierre, 12, from New South Wales, made some top dishes throughout the series, including herbed lamb cutlets and chilli duck wontons, but it was his lamb Wellington that really stole the show. Pierre was named the winner of the Invention Test in Episode Four with this fantastic dish. Gary said, "You should be thrilled – that looks a million bucks!"

about
CHICKEN

LESSON 15
Trussing a chicken

✴ Trussing (or tying) a chicken allows the whole chicken to cook evenly throughout.

✴ To truss a chicken, first rinse the chicken under cold running water, then pat dry with paper towel.

✴ Place the chicken on a chopping board with the breast side up. Bend the joints of the wings back to tuck the wings under the chicken.

✴ Tie the legs together with unwaxed kitchen string. Cross string over the legs and diagonally over the body, then over and under the wings. Wrap the string under the body, then tie in a bow at the legs to secure.

When you truss a chicken, it roasts evenly – and those pesky wings don't dry out!

LESSON 16
How to butterfly and flatten a chicken

STEP 1 Using poultry shears or kitchen scissors, cut the chicken along each side of the back bone, then remove and discard the back bone.

STEP 2 Turn the chicken over so it is breast side-up. Using the heel of your hand, press down firmly on the breastbone of the chicken to flatten it.

Chef's tip A butterflied chicken is great if you're short on time, or want to cook your chook on the barbie, as it's thinner than a regular chicken and cooks through quickly. Try it with our herby marinade on page 54.

LESSON 17
The skewer test

To test if a chicken is cooked through, insert a skewer into the thickest part of the leg, then pull it out and wait for the juices to rise to the surface. If the juices run clear, the chicken is done.

Honey, Chicken & Vegie Kebabs with Couscous

MAKES 12
PREPARATION 20 MINS
COOKING 30 MINS

For this recipe, you'll need 12 x 25cm bamboo skewers. Soak them before using (see Soaking Skewers, opposite).

24 (about 300g) button
  mushrooms
2 large zucchinis
1 large yellow
  or red capsicum
3 x 200g chicken
  breast fillets
24 (about 250g) large
  cherry tomatoes

200g (1 cup) couscous
1½ tbs olive oil

Honey marinade
90g (¼ cup) honey
60ml (¼ cup) olive oil
70g (¼ cup) tomato
  ketchup
2 tsp wholegrain mustard

STEP 1
Preparing mushrooms
Using paper towel or a small pastry brush, remove any dirt from the mushrooms. Don't wash the mushrooms in water, as this will make them soggy. Grip a mushroom in one hand, then, holding a sharp knife in the other hand, trim a little bit off the end of the stalk. Repeat with the remaining mushrooms.

MY SCORE / 10

Mix it up
Have fun with your kebabs. For variations, try using pork, beef or fish instead of chicken, and include hard vegies, such as pumpkin and potato. For the hard vegies, you'll need to peel, cut and cook them three-quarters through in boiling water before skewering. You could also try barbecue sauce instead of tomato for the marinade.

STEP 2
Cutting vegies and chicken
Using a sharp knife, trim the ends of the zucchinis. Using the bridge technique (see Lesson #2, page 7), cut zucchinis and capsicum in half lengthwise. Remove the capsicum stalk and seeds, and discard. Using the bridge and claw techniques (see Lesson #2, page 7), cut the capsicum, zucchinis and chicken into 3cm pieces. Place the chicken in a bowl.

STEP 3
Threading skewers
Hold a bamboo skewer with its pointy end away from you. Carefully push zucchini, capsicum, tomato, chicken and mushroom through the skewers, adding more pieces, but leaving enough room at either end of the skewer so it's easy for you to hold it when cooking and eating. Repeat with the remaining skewers, vegetables and chicken, alternating the ingredients for different combinations. Place the kebabs in a roasting pan and season with salt and pepper.

STEP 4
Marinating and cooking
Preheat oven to 190C. To make the marinade, combine honey, oil, tomato ketchup and mustard in a bowl. Using a pastry brush, brush kebabs on all sides with marinade and set aside at room temperature for 10 minutes to marinate. Transfer pan to oven and roast for 8 minutes. Using oven gloves, carefully remove pan from oven (get an adult to help you). Using tongs, turn kebabs over. Spoon over marinade in pan, then return to the oven for 10 minutes or until the chicken is cooked.

STEP 5
Making couscous
Boil a kettle of water. Place the couscous in a large bowl. Measure 180ml (¾ cup) boiling water and carefully add water to the bowl of couscous (get an adult to help you). Add the olive oil. Using a small spoon, stir to combine. Cover the bowl with plastic wrap and set aside for 10 minutes or until the liquid is completely absorbed. Remove the plastic wrap. Using a fork, fluff couscous and separate grains. Divide couscous among bowls and top with kebabs to serve.

SKILL 2
Soaking skewers
To prevent skewers from burning while cooking, place them in a flat tray, cover with water and leave for 20 minutes. Drain.

Mango Chicken Salad

SERVES **4**
PREPARATION **20 MINS**
COOKING **30 MINS**

3 x 200g chicken breast
   fillets
2 bay leaves
1 sprig rosemary
6 black peppercorns
1 tbs sunflower oil
1 small onion
2 tsp mild curry powder
2 tsp tomato purée
80g (¼ cup) mango
   chutney
70g (¼ cup) Greek-style
   yoghurt
120g (½ cup) sour cream
1 ripe mango
2 stalks celery
2 baby cos lettuce, leaves
   separated, washed
Lime wedges, to serve

MY SCORE   /10

STEP 1
Poaching the chicken
Place the chicken in a deep frying pan and cover with water. Add the bay leaves, rosemary and peppercorns. Bring to a simmer over low–medium heat. Cover pan with a lid and poach gently for 15 minutes or until chicken is cooked through. Remove pan from the heat and allow to cool.

STEP 2
Preparing the onions
Using the bridge and claw techniques (see Lesson #2, page 7), cut the onion in half lengthwise, then finely dice. Heat oil in a saucepan over low heat. Add the onion and cook, stirring, for 8 minutes or until soft. Add curry powder and cook, stirring, for 2 minutes. It's important to cook the curry powder before adding the other ingredients as this mellows the taste of the spices.

STEP 3
Making the dressing
Remove the pan from the heat and add tomato purée, lemon juice, mango chutney and 125ml (½ cup) water. Place the pan over low heat and simmer gently for 15 minutes, stirring occasionally, or until the sauce is thick. Remove from the heat and set aside to cool.

STEP 4
Serving the salad
Place the yoghurt and sour cream in a bowl and stir together. Add cooled curry mixture, season with pepper, then gently stir together. Using the bridge technique, cut chicken into 2cm strips, then into cubes. Cut the celery into 1cm strips, then into cubes. Cut mango into cubes (see Lesson #25, page 129). Add chicken to sauce and gently stir to combine. Arrange lettuce, mango and celery on a platter or in 4 bowls, then spoon over chicken and sauce. Serve with lime wedges.

ROYAL TREATMENT
This is our light and bright version of a British classic, coronation chicken. Created in 1953 to celebrate the coronation of Queen Elizabeth II, this dish is traditionally a blend of poached chicken in a curry mayonnaise. Here we've added crunchy lettuce and celery, and cooling cubes of mango for a refreshing summer salad.

One-pan Roast Chicken with Potatoes and Carrots

SERVES 4
PREPARATION 30 MINS
COOKING 55 MINS

500g small waxy potatoes
  (such as kipfler),
  scrubbed
1 large red onion
1 bunch baby (Dutch)
  carrots
2 tbs honey
60ml (¼ cup) olive oil
8 chicken pieces (use
  a combination of
  drumsticks, marylands
  and breasts)
2 tbs chopped rosemary
2 tbs thyme leaves
2 tbs chopped flat-leaf
  parsley
2 cloves garlic, crushed

STEP 1
Preparing the vegetables
Preheat oven to 200C. Using the bridge technique (see Lesson #2, page 7), cut potatoes in half lengthwise. Peel the onions (see Skill 1, page 20), then, using the bridge technique, cut into thin wedges. Trim and peel the carrots.

STEP 3
Arranging the vegetables
Place the potatoes, onions and carrots in a single layer in a large ovenproof dish – this will help the vegetables cook evenly. Combine the honey and 1 tbs oil and drizzle over the vegetables.

STEP 4
Baking the chicken
Place chicken, skin-side up, over the vegetables. Combine the rosemary, thyme, parsley, garlic and remaining 2 tbs oil in a bowl, then brush over the chicken. Roast for 50 minutes or until the chicken is golden and cooked through. (To see if the chicken is cooked, see Lesson 17, page 79.) Check the potatoes and onions are cooked – a knife should cut a piece of potato easily.

Cooking the chicken and veg in one pan makes everything extra yummy – and saves on washing up!

MY SCORE /10

Wow, this is a magnificently balanced green curry. The heat's slow-generating and the beans are cooked but not squeaky. Clever boy.

GEORGE CALOMBARIS

MY SCORE   /10

Jack's
Thai Green Curry with Coconut Rice

SERVES 4
PREPARATION 20 MINS
COOKING 20 MINS

1 tbs peanut oil
8 chicken thigh fillets,
   trimmed, cut into
   3cm pieces
300ml coconut cream
175g green beans,
   trimmed, halved
4 kaffir lime leaves*
1 tbs fish sauce
1 tsp caster sugar
Coriander sprigs, Thai basil
   leaves* and lime wedges,
   to serve

Coconut rice

2 cups (400g) jasmine
   rice, rinsed, drained
2 x 400ml cans
   coconut milk

Curry paste (makes 1 cup)

4 long green chillies,
   seeded, chopped
3cm piece ginger, peeled,
   finely grated
2 stalks lemongrass, white
   part only, finely chopped
4 kaffir lime leaves,
   roughly chopped
4 cloves garlic,
   finely chopped
2 eschalots,
   finely chopped
¼ cup finely chopped
   Thai basil
1 tbs peanut oil

STEP 1 To make coconut rice, place rice in a large saucepan. Add coconut milk and ¼ tsp salt, and slowly bring to the boil over medium heat. Cover with a lid, reduce heat to low and cook for 10 minutes or until rice has absorbed liquid. Remove from heat and stand, covered, for a further 10 minutes or until rice is tender.

STEP 2 Meanwhile, to make curry paste, place all ingredients in a food processor with ¼ tsp and 2 tbs water. Cover, then process until it forms a smooth paste.

STEP 3 Heat 1 tbs oil in a wok or large, deep frying pan over medium–high heat. Add ½ cup of the curry paste and cook, stirring, for 1 minute or until fragrant. Add the chicken and cook, stirring, for 4 minutes or until chicken is browned and almost cooked through. Add coconut cream, beans and lime leaves, and stir to combine. Simmer, stirring, for 2 minutes or until chicken is cooked through. Add fish sauce and sugar, and stir to combine.

STEP 4 Divide the rice among 4 bowls, top with the curry, then garnish with coriander sprigs and Thai basil. Serve with lime wedges. The remaining curry paste will keep, covered in the fridge, for 7 days.
✳Kaffir lime leaves and Thai basil are from greengrocers and Asian grocers.

ABOUT JACK

Congratulations to Jack, 12, from Tasmania, who was named runner-up of Junior MasterChef. Jack knocked the judges' socks off when he dished up this Thai green curry in the Hot and Cold Elimination in Episode Eight. "Dad went to a cooking school in Thailand, and when he got home he showed us this massively good green curry," says Jack. "He taught me how to make it, and now is my time to show it off."

That is the best dish I've
tasted so far – you've cooked
the duck perfectly.
You're a pocket dynamo!

GARY MEHIGAN

MY SCORE   /10

Nick's Chilli-salt Duck with Bok Choy

SERVES 4
PREPARATION 25 MINS
COOKING 15 MINS

4 x 200g duck breasts, skin on
2 tbs plain flour
2 tsp chilli powder
¼ tsp chilli flakes
80ml (⅓ cup) peanut oil
1 bunch bok choy, trimmed, quartered lengthwise
2 tbs oyster sauce
¼ tsp sesame oil
2 small red chillies, sliced on the diagonal
2 spring onions, sliced on the diagonal
Lemon wedges, to serve

STEP 1 Place a large bamboo steamer over a large saucepan of boiling water. Place duck breasts on a heatproof plate, skin-side up, then place inside steamer and cover with a lid. Reduce heat to low–medium, then steam for 10 minutes or until duck breasts are almost cooked through. Remove the steamer from the pan (get an adult to help you). Rest the duck for 15 minutes.

STEP 2 Combine the flour, chilli powder, chilli flakes and some salt and pepper in a bowl. Pat the duck breasts dry with paper towel, then coat well in the flour mixture.

STEP 3 Heat 60ml (¼ cup) peanut oil in large frying pan over high heat. Cook duck, skin-side down, for 3 minutes or until fat has rendered (melted). Turn and cook for 2 minutes or until golden but still pink in the centre. Rest, loosely covered with foil, for 5 minutes.

STEP 4 Meanwhile, heat remaining 1 tbs peanut oil in a wok over medium–high heat. Add bok choy and cook, tossing, for 1 minute or until wilted. Add oyster sauce and sesame oil, then toss to coat.

STEP 5 To serve, divide the bok choy among 4 plates. Thickly slice duck on the diagonal and arrange on top of bok choy. Scatter over chilli and spring onions, then serve with lemon wedges.

ABOUT NICK

Ten-year-old Nick, from New South Wales, proved that he's a whiz in the kitchen with his chocolate fondant pudding, crispy-skinned chicken and this awesome Asian chilli-salt duck from Episode Seven. When he tasted it, George Calombaris said, "I'm not going to tell you how much I liked this dish, I'm going to write it down so you can keep it: I love it. Number 1."

FLOUR

Measuring & sifting

MEASURING When measuring dry ingredients such as flour or sugar, level your spoon and cup measurements off with a knife or spatula. Be fussy about getting the right amount: when it comes to baking, more isn't better.

SIFTING Sifting breaks up any clumps and adds air to the flour, helping to produce lighter cakes and pastries. When you're baking sponge cakes, you sift the flour three times! Years ago, it was also done to remove impurities.

Testing if a cake is ready

CAKES Using oven gloves, remove the cake from the oven, gently insert a skewer through the centre of the cake to the bottom of the pan. Slowly pull out the skewer: if the skewer is clean the cake is done; if the skewer has uncooked batter on it, cook the cake further.

CUPCAKES For cupcakes, you can usually tell if they are cooked through if they are golden and feel springy to touch. If you are unsure, use a skewer as above.

SPONGES With a sponge cake, it's better to go by appearance and feel – piercing with a skewer will deflate it. Towards the end of baking time, open the oven gently: it should be well risen, browned and not shrunken from the side of the pan. Feel the top of the cake: it should be slightly springy. Immediately turn out sponge onto a wire rack, as it will continue to cook and dry out if left in the pan. Quickly invert it onto a plate to prevent the wire racks marking the cake.

Separating eggs

✳ Using a single, sharp movement, crack egg on the side of a bowl or with a knife, as close to the middle of the shell as possible. Holding egg in both hands over a bowl, use your thumbs to gently break shell in half.

✳ Turn shells upright and allow white to fall into bowl. Tilt shells towards each other and slip yolk from one shell to the other so remaining white falls into the bowl, taking care not to break yolk. Continue until only yolk remains. Tip yolk into a separate bowl.

Shortcrust Pastry

PREPARATION 5 MINS

Shortcrust is a type of pastry that has a crumbly texture (unlike puff pastry, which is more flaky). It's fun to make, and once you've learned how, you can make so many things, such as savoury piggies in blankets (see recipe, page 94) and sweet lemon tarts (opposite). Allow an extra 30 minutes to chill pastry.

125g cold unsalted butter
250g (1²⁄₃ cups) plain flour, plus extra, to dust

STEP 1
Preparing butter and flour
Using the bridge technique (see Lesson #2, page 7), roughly chop butter (the pieces don't have to be even). Place the butter and flour in the bowl of a food processor, taking care not to touch the sharp blade. Place the lid on the food processor, then press the start button and process until the mixture looks like breadcrumbs (get an adult to help you operate the food processor).

STEP 2
Processing pastry
Remove the lid. Measure 60ml (¼ cup) iced water and drizzle water over the mixture in the food processor. Replace the lid. Using the pulse button, process the mixture in short bursts (this prevents the pastry from being overworked and becoming tough). Stop processing just as the pastry starts to come together, but hasn't quite formed a ball. Tip out pastry onto a clean, floured work surface.

STEP 3
Chilling pastry
Using floured hands, press the pastry together to form a ball, then flatten the ball slightly. Avoid over-handling the pastry as it will become warm and soft. Wrap the pastry in plastic wrap and refrigerate for 30 minutes or until needed. Lightly dust a sheet of baking paper and rolling pin with flour. Place dough on the paper, then, pressing rolling pin gently, roll out away from you to the desired thickness.

Did you know? Flour can be made from all sorts of things, not just wheat. Ground almonds are a form of flour called meal and can be used in cakes. Cornflour is used for thickening. Rice is also ground into a flour and is used in Asian cooking.

LEMON TARTS

Preheat oven to 200C. Grease a 12-hole patty pan, then lightly dust a sheet of baking paper and a rolling pin with flour. Place 1 quantity shortcrust pastry on paper. Using the rolling pin, roll away from you until the pastry is 3mm thick. Using a floured 7cm pastry cutter, cut 12 rounds and use to line holes. Using a fork, prick bases of tart shells. Bake for 12 minutes until dry and golden. Cool slightly. Fill each tart with 1 tbs ready-made lemon curd. Dust with icing sugar to serve. Makes 12.

MY SCORE   /10

Piggies in Blankets

MAKES 24
PREPARATION 25 MINS
COOKING 25 MINS

Also known as 'little fingers', chipolatas are small sausages. To make them 'piggie'-sized, roll them first on a work surface using your hands. This will make them easier to twist and divide in half. Before starting this recipe, you'll also need to make, then chill, the pastry, so allow an extra 30 minutes.

12 pork or beef chipolata sausages
Plain flour, to dust
1 quantity shortcrust pastry (see recipe, page 92)
½ cup ready-made pesto
1 egg, lightly beaten
Sesame seeds, to sprinkle
Tomato ketchup, to serve

These little piggies... love tomato ketchup! Super-dunk them, or use ketchup instead of pesto for an extra burst of sweetness.

MY SCORE /10

STEP 1

Cooking sausages
Preheat grill to high.
To make piggie-sized
sausages, twist in half
at the centre and, using
scissors, cut in half. Place
on an oven tray. Grill for
4 minutes. Using oven
gloves, carefully remove
tray and turn sausages
over with tongs. Return
to the grill for a further
4 minutes until browned all
over. Remove from the grill
and cool for 10 minutes.

STEP 2

Rolling out pastry
Lightly dust a sheet of
baking paper and rolling
pin with flour. Using bridge
technique (see Lesson #2,
page 7), cut pastry into
24 equal portions. Place
1 portion on the paper,
then, pressing rolling pin
gently, roll out away from
you to form a long strip
big enough to wrap around
a sausage. Repeat with the
remaining portions, dusting
with flour each time.

STEP 3

Wrapping the sausages
Preheat oven to 180C.
Line 2 oven trays with
baking paper. Spread 1 tsp
pesto over each pastry
strip, leaving a thin border.
Place a sausage on each
strip across one end and
roll up to enclose. Press
the edges along the join
and ends to seal and cover
sausage. Repeat with
the remaining strips and
sausages, then transfer
to the lined oven trays.

STEP 4

**Baking piggies in
blankets**
To glaze the pastry, using
a pastry brush, brush with
egg, then sprinkle with
sesame seeds. Transfer
to the oven and bake for
8 minutes. Using oven
gloves, carefully swap trays
for even colour, then bake
for a further 7 minutes
or until golden. Remove
from oven. (Get an adult to
help.) Serve with ketchup.

**Chef's tip To prevent
pastry from becoming
soft, place rolled-out
strips on a tray in the
fridge until ready to use.**

Spice it up
Have a little fun with your
piggies in blankets. For a
variation, try poppy, fennel
or caraway seeds, or finely
grated parmesan, instead
of sesame seeds in step 4.

Basic White Bread

MAKES 1 LOAF
PREPARATION 105 MINS
COOKING 40 MINS

450g (3 cups) strong plain
flour, plus extra,
to dust
2 x 7g sachets dried yeast
2 tbs olive oil

STEP 1
Mixing the dough
Place the flour in a bowl and sprinkle over the yeast. Make a well in the centre of the flour. Mix the oil into 150ml warm water and pour into the well. Using a wooden spoon, slowly bring the flour into the centre until it comes together into a soft dough that leaves the bowl clean.

STEP 2
Kneading the dough
Sprinkle a little flour over a work surface. Turn the dough out onto the surface, then knead the dough by pushing it down and away with the heel of your hand. Pull the dough back with your fingers, then push it back on the work surface. Turn dough slightly and keep kneading for 8 minutes or until the dough has a smooth and elastic texture.

STEP 3
Baking the bread
Grease a 23cm loaf pan with butter and sprinkle with flour. Place dough in pan, cover, then leave to rise in a warm place for 40 minutes or until doubled in size. Preheat oven to 220C. Bake bread for 20 minutes or until golden. To test if it is cooked, using oven gloves, remove loaf from pan (get an adult to help you) and tap the base – it should sound hollow.

Flour power

Strong plain flour is also known as baker's flour. This type is ideal for making bread as it contains more protein (or gluten) than regular plain flour. The added protein helps the dough to rise evenly, giving your bread a lovely light texture.

Plain flour can be used for making pastries and thickening sauces or in any other foods that don't need to rise. **Self-raising flour** contains a raising agent and is used for making dishes that need to rise, such as cakes and puddings.

MY SCORE /10

Pick & Mix Pizzas

MAKES 2 PIZZAS
PREPARATION 30 MINS
COOKING 60 MINS

10 ripe tomatoes, halved
3 cloves garlic, unpeeled
2 tbs olive oil,
    plus extra, to grease
150g sliced salami
200g baby bocconcini,
    halved
75g (½ cup) pitted
    kalamata olives
½ cup basil leaves
Plain flour, to dust
1 quantity of bread dough
    (see recipe p 96)

MY SCORE   /10

STEP 1
Roasting the tomatoes
Preheat oven to 200C. Place the tomatoes, cut side-up, in a roasting pan with the garlic, drizzle with oil and roast for 40 minutes or until the tomatoes are soft.

STEP 2
Making the sauce
Let the tomatoes cool slightly. Using a wooden spoon, push the tomatoes through a sieve into a bowl to make a thick sauce. Discard the skin and seeds left in the sieve. Squeeze the soft garlic cloves out of their skins and stir into the tomatoes. If you don't have time to roast the tomatoes, use passata (sieved puréed tomatoes) instead.

STEP 3
Preparing the pizza bases
Grease 2 oven trays with a little olive oil (or see Chef's Tip). Lightly dust a work surface and a rolling pin with flour. Halve the dough and place one half on the work surface. Using the rolling pin, roll away from you to form a 25cm round. Repeat with the remaining dough. Place pizza bases onto the greased trays.

STEP 4
Spreading the sauce over the base
Spread the sieved tomato and garlic sauce over the pizza bases – it's easiest to do this with the back of a spoon. You will need about 80ml (⅓ cup) of sauce for each pizza base. Any leftover sauce will keep in the fridge for 1 week.

STEP 5
Topping the pizza
Top the pizza bases with salami, bocconcini, olives and basil. Bake in the oven for 15 minutes or until golden.

Chef's tip Instead of oiling the trays, you can put a piece of baking paper on each tray and sprinkle with polenta (cornmeal) – this adds flavour and makes it easier to slide the pizza off the tray.

For speedy pizza, try using pita bread instead.

Topping mad
Once you've made your base, you can add any toppings you like! Try sliced ham, pineapple and grated cheddar, or a super cheesy pizza with blue cheese, parmesan and mozzarella.

This goes to show that simplicity wins the day. That is the best doughnut I've ever tasted.

GARY MEHIGAN

MY SCORE /10

Sofia's
Italian Doughnuts

MAKES 16
PREPARATION 30 MINS
COOKING 20 MINS

2 beurre bosc pears,
   peeled, cored
1 tsp grated lime zest,
   plus 2 tbs lime juice
110g (½ cup) caster sugar
2 tbs passionfruit pulp
1 egg, lightly beaten
1 tsp vanilla bean paste
300g (2 cups) self-raising
   flour, sifted
Sunflower oil,
   to shallow-fry
125g punnet blueberries
2 tbs honey

Crème pâtissière
225ml milk
½ tsp vanilla bean paste
3 egg yolks
75g (⅓ cup) caster sugar
1½ tbs cornflour

STEP 1 For the crème pâtissière, place milk and vanilla paste in a saucepan over medium heat and bring to just below boiling point. Remove from the heat.
STEP 2 Whisk yolks and sugar together until thick and pale. Add cornflour and whisk until combined. Slowly whisk the milk mixture into the egg mixture until well combined (get an adult to help you). Transfer to a clean saucepan. Whisk over medium heat for 3 minutes or until mixture thickens. Transfer to a bowl, cover surface with plastic wrap to prevent a skin forming, then chill until cold.
STEP 3 To make the doughnuts, using a box grater, grate the pear and place in a large bowl with the lime zest and juice, sugar, passionfruit pulp, egg, vanilla paste, 250ml (1 cup) water and a pinch of salt, then stir to combine. Gradually mix in sifted flour to form a wet dough.
STEP 4 Fill a deep frying pan with 2cm of oil. Heat over medium heat until 180C (or a cube of bread turns golden in 10 seconds). In batches of 4, gently drop heaped tablespoons of dough into oil and top with 3 blueberries (get an adult to help you). Cook for 1½ minutes each side or until golden and puffed. Drain on paper towel. Repeat with remaining mixture.
STEP 5 Place crème pâtissière in a piping bag. Push the tip of the nozzle into the base of each doughnut and pipe about 1 tsp crème pâtissière into each.
STEP 6 Warm the honey with 1 tbs water in a small saucepan until runny. Place the doughnuts on a platter, then drizzle with honey and serve.

ABOUT SOFIA

Twelve-year-old Queenslander Sofia entered the competition with her twin sister, Isabella, impressing the judges with the Italian and Sicilian cuisine taught to them by their mum and *nonna*. Sofia won the Mystery Box Challenge in Episode 13 with these Italian-style doughnuts called pettole. "This dish comes from Puglia, in the heel of Italy, and my family makes a similar dish in Sicily, called sfinge."

about
SUGAR

LESSON 21
Lining cake pans

ROUND Grease base and sides of the pan by spraying with a light coating of cooking oil or brushing with melted butter. Place cake pan on a sheet of baking paper and trace around it, then cut just inside the line to allow for the thickness of the pan so it will fit the inside base. If you need to line the sides as well, measure the depth and circumference of the pan, then cut a panel of paper to fit.
RECTANGULAR OR SQUARE Mark the width of the pan on baking paper, then cut a strip that wide, which is long enough to line the pan from end to end, allowing an extra 5cm on each end as overhang. Mark the length of the pan on a second piece of baking paper, then cut another strip to line the pan from side to side, again allowing for overhang. Place strips in the greased pan, overlapping. Use overhanging baking paper to ease the cake out of the pan.

LESSON 22
Blind baking

STEP 1
Preheat oven to 190C. Line a tart pan with a removable base with pastry, then prick the base with a fork. Line the base and sides of the uncooked pastry with baking paper and fill with rice, dried beans or metal or ceramic baking weights. (This stops the pastry base rising during cooking.)

STEP 2
Place on an oven tray and bake in the oven for 12 minutes. Using oven gloves, remove the pan from the oven, then remove the paper and rice (get an adult to help you). Bake for a further 10 minutes (depending on the size of the case) or until dry and light golden. Remove from oven and cool completely before filling.

Blind-baking your pastry before adding the filling prevents the base becoming soggy.

Pear & Berry Cake

SERVES **6**
PREPARATION **20 MINS**
COOKING **45 MINS**

1 orange
185g unsalted butter,
   softened, plus extra,
   to grease
165g (¾ cup) caster sugar,
   plus 1 tbs extra
3 eggs
185g (1¼ cups) self-raising
   flour
2 ripe pears
150g (1 cup) fresh or
   frozen berries
Icing sugar, to dust

*Always leave
the cake to cool
for 10 minutes
in the pan to
help it set.*

MY SCORE   /10

STEP 1
Grating the zest

Preheat oven to 170C. Grease and line base and sides of a 20cm springform pan (see Lesson #21, page 103). Using a box grater, hold top of grater firmly with one hand. With your other hand, hold orange at top end of grater and push down the side with the smallest holes – avoid grating the bitter white pith. Using a pastry brush, remove zest from grater, then place in a bowl.

STEP 2
Beating the butter and sugar

Add butter and sugar to bowl of zest. Using electric beaters, beat butter and sugar until pale and fluffy. Add 1 egg and beat well. Continue beating in eggs one at a time, adding a little flour to prevent the mixture from separating.

Chef's tip Keep your eggs at room temperature – this will make your cake light and airy.

STEP 3
Sifting flour into mixture

Sift the remaining flour over the mixture. Using a spatula, carefully fold the mixture together until combined. Using a spatula, scrape the mixture from the sides of the bowl into the centre. Spoon just over half of the mixture into the cake pan. Peel the pears. Using the bridge technique (see Lesson #2, page 7), cut the pears into quarters. Remove the core and stalk, then thinly slice the pears. Place the pears in a bowl with the extra sugar and gently toss to combine.

STEP 4
Baking the cake

Scatter pears and berries over the cake mixture in the pan, then dollop the remaining mixture on top – it doesn't matter if the fruit isn't completely covered. Bake on the middle shelf of the oven for 25 minutes. Using oven gloves, remove cake pan from oven and cover with baking paper to prevent cake browning too much (get an adult to help you). Return the cake to the oven for a further 20 minutes or until golden and cooked through. To check if cake is cooked, push a skewer into the centre of the cake (get an adult to help). It should come out clean, without any uncooked mixture stuck to it. Cool in the pan for 10 minutes, then unclip the pan and slide the cake onto a wire rack. Dust with icing sugar and serve.

Quick Vanilla Biscuits

MY SCORE ____ /10

MAKES 30
PREPARATION 20 MINS
COOKING 20 MINS

125g cold unsalted butter
40g (¼ cup) icing sugar
2 tsp vanilla extract
150g (1 cup) plain flour
35g (¼ cup) cornflour
2 tsp sugar

STEP 1
Making the dough

Using a box grater, hold the top of the grater firmly with one hand. With your other hand, hold the cold butter at the top of the grater and push down the side of the grater with the largest holes. Place grated butter in a large bowl with icing sugar and vanilla extract. Beat with a wooden spoon or electric mixer until combined. Sift flour and cornflour together over the butter mixture. Beat with a wooden spoon or electric mixer on the lowest speed until combined and the dough is smooth.

STEP 2
Shaping the dough

Turn the dough out onto a lightly floured surface, then, using floured hands, bring the dough together. Halve the dough and shape into discs, then wrap each piece in plastic wrap. Refrigerate for 45 minutes or until firm enough to roll.

STEP 3
Rolling and cutting the dough

Preheat oven to 160C. Line 2 oven trays with baking paper. Lightly dust a sheet of baking paper and a rolling pin with flour. Place 1 portion of dough on the paper, then, pressing rolling pin gently, roll out away from you until it is 1cm thick. Use a 5.5cm biscuit cutter to stamp out shapes (see Chef's Tip). Re-roll leftover dough and repeat. Place on trays and lightly sprinkle the biscuits with sugar. Repeat with the remaining dough. (You should be able to make about 30 biscuits.)

STEP 4
Baking the biscuits

Bake the biscuits in the oven for 10 minutes. Using oven gloves, carefully swap the trays on the shelves (get an adult to help you), then bake for a further 10 minutes or until the biscuits are light golden and cooked through. Remove the biscuits from the oven and set aside to cool on the trays for 5 minutes. Transfer to a wire rack to cool completely.

Chef's tip **Dipping the biscuit cutter in flour makes it easier to cut the dough.**

Creative cookies

* Fold in ⅓ cup sultanas, M&M's Minis or chocolate chips after you've beaten in the flour.
* Use different biscuit cutters for Christmas or Halloween.
* Ice the cooled biscuits with melted chocolate, then decorate with sprinkles or cachous.
* Sandwich biscuits with ganache (see Lesson #23, page 117).

Fruit & Nut Muffins

SERVES **12 MUFFINS**
PREPARATION **15 MINS**
COOKING **25 MINS**

Butter, to grease
1 orange
1 ripe banana, peeled
60g (½ cup) pecans,
    chopped
50g (⅓ cup) Craisins*
300g (2 cups) self-raising
    flour
2 tsp baking powder
110g (½ firmly packed cup)
    brown sugar
2 eggs
95g (⅓ cup) plain yoghurt
125ml (½ cup)
    full-cream milk
1 tsp vanilla extract
50ml sunflower oil

MY SCORE   / 10

STEP 1
Preparing the fruit

Preheat oven to 190C. Line a 12-hole (80ml) muffin pan with butter and line with paper cases. Using a box grater, hold the top of the grater firmly with one hand. With your other hand, hold the orange at the top end of the grater and push down the side of the grater with the smallest holes – try to avoid grating the bitter white pith. Using a pastry brush, remove the zest from the grater, then place in a bowl. Add the banana and mash well with a fork. Juice half the orange, then add juice to the bowl with the pecans and Craisins.

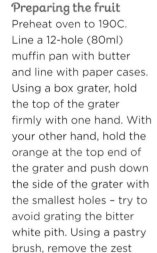

Chef's tip To make light, moist muffins, it's important not to overmix the batter – the mixture should still have some lumps in it.

STEP 2
Sifting the dry ingredients

Using a sieve, sift the flour and baking powder into a large bowl. Add the sugar and stir together. Crack the eggs into a separate bowl and whisk with a fork. Add the yoghurt, milk, vanilla and oil to the beaten egg and mix well.

STEP 3
Combining the wet and dry ingredients

Pour egg mixture into flour mixture. Using a spatula, quickly and gently stir everything together – don't overmix or your muffins will be tough (see Chef's Tip). Add the fruit and nut mixture and quickly stir together. Remember, don't overmix – you just want to stir in the fruit mixture.

STEP 4
Baking the muffins

Spoon the mixture into the muffin holes until three-quarters full. Bake for 25 minutes or until risen and golden. Cool in the pan for 5 minutes, then place on a wire rack to cool completely.
✳ Craisins is a brand of dried, sweetened cranberries available from supermarkets.

Mix & match muffins

Swap pecans and Craisins for these combinations:
Apple & hazelnut Handful of chopped hazelnuts; 2 apples, peeled, cored and finely chopped; grated zest of 1 lemon and juice of ½ lemon.
Pear & raisin Handful of raisins; 2 pears, peeled, cored and finely chopped; grated zest of 1 lemon and juice of ½ lemon.
Apricot & pecan Handful of chopped pecans; 400g can apricots, drained and chopped.

Apple & Berry Crumble

Fruit crumbles are super-easy to make and the best thing about them is that the messier they are, the yummier they look!

SERVES 4–6
PREPARATION 20 MINS
COOKING 35 MINS

1 orange
6 golden delicious apples
500g packet frozen
    mixed berries
55g (¼ cup firmly packed)
    dark brown sugar
1 tbs plain flour
Vanilla ice-cream, to serve

Crumble topping
125g cold unsalted butter,
    plus extra, to grease
185g (1¼ cups) plain flour
½ tsp ground cinnamon
75g (⅓ cup firmly packed)
    dark brown sugar
110g (1¼ cups) rolled oats
20g (¼ cup) flaked
    almonds

MY SCORE   /10

STEP 1
Preparing flour and butter

Preheat oven to 200C. Grease a 1.5L (6-cup) ovenproof dish with butter. To make crumble topping, using a sieve, sift the flour with cinnamon into a large bowl. Using the bridge and claw techniques (see Lesson #2, page 7), roughly chop butter (the pieces don't have to be even). Avoid over-handling the butter (see Chef's Tip).

STEP 2
Combining butter and flour

Add the butter to the flour mixture. Using the same knife, cut the butter until roughly quartered. Using your fingertips, gently rub the butter between the tips of your thumbs and fingers, so the butter flattens and combines with the flour. While rubbing, lift your fingers above bowl to allow air to cool butter (see Chef's Tip).

STEP 3
Finishing crumble topping

Holding bowl with two hands, gently shake bowl to make any remaining large pieces of butter come to the top. Continue rubbing in butter until the mixture looks like coarse breadcrumbs. Using a large spoon, stir in the sugar, oats and almonds.

Chef's tip To prevent the topping from becoming greasy, work quickly; the heat from your hands melts the butter rapidly. If the butter melts, place mixture in the fridge for 5 minutes, then continue.

STEP 4
Zesting and juicing orange

Using an orange zester (as pictured) or the smallest holes of a box grater, grate the rind of the orange (see page 11 for more on grating). Using the bridge technique, cut the orange in half. Place 1 orange half, flesh-side down, over a juicer. Press down firmly, then twist to release the juice. Repeat with the remaining half. Place juice and zest in a large bowl, discarding seeds and flesh.

STEP 5
Preparing fruit and baking

Preheat oven to 200C. Using a vegetable peeler, peel apples. Using bridge technique, cut the apples in half. Remove cores (see page 117). Using the claw technique, cut halves into 2cm pieces. Add apples to orange mixture, then add berries, sugar and flour. Toss to combine with your hands. Spoon mixture into the greased dish and scatter with topping. Place on bottom shelf of oven and bake for 35 minutes or until the top is golden and juices are bubbling. Using oven gloves, remove from oven. (Get an adult to help.) Cool for 10 minutes. Serve with ice-cream.

Ready to crumble!

Get creative with your crumbles. For a variation, try our yummy peach melba crumble. Substitute your favourite muesli for the rolled oats, and shredded coconut for the almonds in step 3. Then, substitute 1kg tub peaches in natural juices, drained, and 500g frozen raspberries for the apples and berries in step 5.

Stuffed Baked Apples

SERVES 6
PREPARATION 15 MINS
COOKING 20 MINS

30g (¼ cup) pecans
35g (¼ cup) dried apricots
55g dark chocolate
  buttons
6 granny smith apples
30g unsalted butter,
  chopped
60ml (¼ cup) pouring
  cream
60ml (¼ cup) maple syrup

STEP 1
Preparing filling
Roughly chop pecans and dried apricots (see Chef's Tip), then combine in a bowl with the chocolate.

STEP 2
Preparing the apples
Halve and core apples (see Skill 3, below) leaving a nice, neat cavity.

Chef's tip Use scissors to cut up the dried fruit.

STEP 3
Filling the apples
Place the cored apple halves, cut-side up, in an ovenproof dish. Spoon the fruit and nut mixture neatly into each apple cavity, mounding it slightly, then press down firmly to keep it in place.

STEP 4
Baking the apples
Preheat oven to 170C. Pour the cream and maple syrup over the apples. Place the dish in the oven and bake for 25 minutes or until the apples are soft. Using oven gloves, remove the dish from the oven (get an adult to help). Remove the apples from the dish and pour the sauce into a jug. Serve the apples with the sauce.

SKILL 3
How to core fruit
To core the apples, using the bridge technique (see Lesson #2, page 7), cut apples in half lengthwise. Using a melon baller or teaspoon, scoop the core from the centre. Or quarter the apples, then, using the claw technique, cut out core.

These baked apples in a sticky maple sauce taste great. Plus, they're a good source of vitamin C, fibre and potassium.

MY SCORE /10

MY SCORE   /10

Lucy's South American Three-milk Puddings

SERVES 6
PREPARATION 25 MINS
COOKING 15 MINS

4 eggs, separated (see
  Lesson #20, page 91)
150g (⅔ cup) caster sugar
90g unsalted butter,
  softened
1 tsp vanilla bean paste
60ml (¼ cup) milk
150g (1 cup) plain flour
1 tsp baking powder
150ml pouring cream
2 tsp icing sugar
2 tbs toasted pistachios,
  finely chopped
Raspberries, to serve

Soaking mixture
160ml (⅔ cup)
  evaporated milk
125ml (½ cup)
  condensed milk
150ml pouring cream

Strawberry coulis
250g strawberries, hulled,
  plus 6 strawberries,
  fanned (see Lesson #27,
  page 129), to serve
1 tbs caster sugar

STEP 1 Preheat oven to 200C. Grease and line the bases of 6 x 1 cup (250ml) dariole moulds with baking paper.
STEP 2 Place egg whites in a large metal bowl. Using an electric mixer, beat until soft peaks form. Add 1 tbs caster sugar and beat until glossy.
STEP 3 Using an electric mixer, beat butter and remaining sugar until thick and pale. Beat in vanilla paste and egg yolks until pale. Add milk, flour and baking powder, then beat until combined.
STEP 4 In 2 batches, use a large metal spoon to fold egg white mixture into the egg mixture until just combined. Divide among prepared moulds and bake for 15 minutes or until a skewer inserted into the centre comes out clean.
STEP 5 Meanwhile, for soaking mixture, whisk ingredients together in a bowl.
STEP 6 For coulis, place berries and sugar in a food processor and whiz until smooth. Strain through a fine sieve to remove the seeds. Set aside.
STEP 7 Whip cream and icing sugar until soft peaks form. Chill until required.
STEP 8 Using a skewer, repeatedly pierce the top of cooked puddings. Pour soaking mixture over warm puddings and place in the fridge for 15 minutes.
STEP 9 To serve, remove puddings from moulds. Top with whipped cream and pistachios. Serve with coulis, a few raspberries and a fanned strawberry.

ABOUT LUCY

Lucy is 11 years old and lives in Victoria. Lucy has a knack for making delicious desserts, including the pretty strawberry sponge in Heat Two of the Top 50, and this pudding in the Hot and Cold Challenge. "This is called tres-leche in Mexican, which means 'three milks'," says Lucy. "I make it for Mum a lot, and I like the texture because it's so moist."

There's a certain feeling that goes through your body when you eat something this tasty. It's just so deliciously moist and full of flavour.
GEORGE CALOMBARIS

about
CHOCOLATE

LESSON 23

Chocolate ganache

* Combine 200g chopped dark chocolate and 200ml pouring cream in a heatproof bowl over a saucepan of barely simmering water (don't let the bowl touch the water). Stir with a spoon until melted and smooth.
* Remove from the heat and cool at room temperature, stirring occasionally until the ganache is thick and spreadable. Use to sandwich biscuits or ice cakes.
* If making truffles (see Lesson #24), allow to cool, then chill in the fridge until set.
* Ganache can be frozen for up to 6 months.

Gently warm the ganache in a pan over low heat, then use as a dip for strawberries, marshmallows or Turkish delight.

LESSON 24

Chocolate truffles

STEP 1

Make a batch of chocolate ganache (see Lesson #23) and chill until firm. Using a teaspoon, scoop out bite-sized pieces of ganache.

STEP 2

Dust your hands with icing sugar to prevent them sticking, then roll the ganache mixture in the palm of your hands to form balls. Roll the balls in toasted coconut or cocoa, then place in mini paper cases, if desired.

No-cook Chocolate Cake

SERVES 10
PREPARATION 20 MINS
SETTING 2 HOURS

200g unsalted butter, softened, plus extra, to grease
20 digestive biscuits or scotch finger biscuits
300g milk chocolate
230g (²/₃ cup) golden syrup
90g (²/₃ cup) Craisins*
45g (¹/₃ cup) roasted pistachio kernels, roughly chopped
35g (¹/₃ cup) roasted walnuts, roughly chopped
Cocoa, to dust

MY SCORE   /10

STEP 1
Breaking the biscuits
Grease a 10cm x 25cm, 6-cup loaf pan with extra butter, then line base and sides with baking paper (see Lesson #21, page 103). Using your hands, break the digestive biscuits into small pieces about the size of a 10 cent coin and place in a large bowl. Set aside until needed.

Chef's tip Golden syrup is sticky, so spray the measuring cup with cooking oil spray before you pour in the syrup.

STEP 2
Making a double saucepan
Choose a medium saucepan and a heatproof bowl that will sit snugly over the top. Half-fill the saucepan with cold water, then place it over high heat and bring to the boil. Reduce heat to low–medium, so the water is at a gentle simmer.

STEP 3
Preparing the chocolate mixture
Break the chocolate into small pieces and place in the heatproof bowl. Using the bridge and claw techniques (see Lesson #2, page 7), cut the butter into small pieces, or break up using a teaspoon. Add to the bowl of chocolate with the golden syrup.

STEP 4
Melting the chocolate mixture
Place the heatproof bowl containing the chocolate mixture over the saucepan of simmering water and leave for 1 minute. Remove the saucepan from the heat (get an adult to help you, as the water is very hot). Using a wooden spoon, stir ingredients together until chocolate and butter are melted and the ingredients are well combined.

STEP 5
Combining and chilling the cake mixture
Add Craisins and nuts to biscuits. Using your hands, toss together to combine. Pour chocolate mixture over biscuit mixture and stir with a wooden spoon until Craisins and nuts are coated in chocolate. The mixture will be quite chunky, so you will need to use a little muscle power to mix it well! Spoon mixture into the lined pan. Using the back of a spoon, press down firmly, so that there are no gaps, then smooth the top using the spoon. Cover the pan with plastic wrap and refrigerate for 2 hours or until very firm. Run a dinner knife around the inside of the pan, then, using the baking paper, pull cake out of pan. Place upside-down on a board, peel away paper, dust with cocoa, then cut into slices.
✳Craisins is a brand of dried, sweetened cranberries available from supermarkets.

Masterclass with Gary
White Chocolate & Cherry Clafoutis

SERVES 2-4
PREPARATION 30 MINS
COOKING 30 MINS

35g unsalted butter,
  melted, plus extra,
  to grease
110g (½ cup) caster sugar,
  plus extra, to dust
50g (⅓ cup) plain flour
1 egg
1 egg yolk
1 lemon, zested
½ tsp vanilla bean paste
80ml (⅓ cup) milk
80ml (⅓ cup) thickened
  cream
60ml (¼ cup) orange juice
50g white chocolate,
  coarsely grated

Marinated cherries
300g cherries
1 tbs caster sugar
1 tbs orange juice

**Cherry & rosewater
compote**
150g cherries
1 orange, zested, juiced
3 tsp maple syrup
½ tsp rosewater*
1 cinnamon quill

Mascarpone cream
1 tsp vanilla bean paste
1 tsp icing sugar,
  plus extra, to dust
150ml thickened cream
85g (⅓ cup) mascarpone
  cheese

STEP 1
Preparing the dishes
Brush 2 x 350ml shallow oval or round ceramic dishes with extra melted butter. Sprinkle evenly with a little extra sugar, then shake out excess sugar.

STEP 2
Marinating the cherries
Pit the cherries (see Lesson #26, page 129), then combine the cherries, sugar and orange juice in a bowl. Set aside for 30 minutes to marinate.

STEP 3
Making the compote
Meanwhile, to make the compote, pit the cherries (see Lesson #26, page 129), then place in a small saucepan with orange zest and juice, maple syrup, rosewater and cinnamon. Bring to a simmer over low-medium heat and cook, stirring occasionally, for 10 minutes or until cherries are soft and liquid is reduced slightly. Remove from the heat and cool.

STEP 4
Making the clafoutis
Preheat oven to 180C. Combine flour and a pinch of salt in a bowl, then make a well in the centre. Whisk in egg, yolk, lemon zest and vanilla until smooth. Combine milk and cream in a small jug. Gradually whisk into flour mixture, in 2 batches, until combined. Add sugar, juice, melted butter and chocolate, then stir until combined.

STEP 5
Baking the clafoutis
Divide marinated cherries and any juices among the prepared dishes, then pour over batter until dishes are three-quarters full. Bake for 30 minutes or until set and tops are golden.

STEP 6

Serving the clafoutis

For the mascarpone cream, using an electric mixer, beat all ingredients together to soft peaks. Dust the clafoutis with icing sugar, then serve with cherry compote and mascarpone cream. ✳ Rosewater is water that's distilled with rose petals to make a fragrant liquid that can be used in cooking. It's available from delis and Middle Eastern grocers.

MY SCORE   /10

Switch the cherries for blueberries, peaches or plums for a fruity twist!

Masterclass with George
Hazelnut & Chocolate Self-saucing Puddings

SERVES 6
PREPARATION 20 MINS
COOKING 14 MINS

50g unsalted butter, melted, cooled, plus extra melted butter, to grease
150g (1 cup) self-raising flour
45g (⅓ cup) roasted peeled hazelnuts, roughly chopped
1½ tbs cocoa powder
55g (¼ firmly packed cup) brown sugar
60g dark chocolate (70% cocoa solids), roughly chopped
150ml milk
1 egg, lightly beaten
Icing sugar and whipped cream, to serve

Candied orange zest
1 orange
55g (¼ cup) caster sugar
60ml (¼ cup) orange juice

Chocolate sauce
110g (½ firmly packed cup) brown sugar
25g (¼ cup) cocoa powder, sifted

STEP 1
Cutting zest into strips
Using a vegetable peeler, peel zest from the orange in long strips, trying to avoid the bitter white pith. Using the claw technique (see Lesson #2, page 7), cut strips of orange zest into thin strips.

STEP 2
Making candied zest
Place orange zest, sugar, juice and 60ml (¼ cup) water in a small saucepan. Stir over low heat until sugar dissolves, then simmer, without stirring, for 15 minutes or until the zest is translucent and liquid is syrupy. Cool.

STEP 3
Making pudding batter
Meanwhile, preheat oven to 190C. Brush 6 x 180ml (¾ cup) ramekins with extra melted butter and place on an oven tray. Combine flour, hazelnuts, cocoa, brown sugar and chocolate in a large bowl and stir to combine. Make a well in the centre and slowly pour in the milk and egg, whisking until combined. Divide batter among ramekins.

STEP 4
Making chocolate sauce
To make chocolate sauce, combine brown sugar, cocoa and 200ml warm water in a jug and stir to dissolve. Carefully pour chocolate sauce over puddings. Bake in the oven for 14 minutes or until the top is firm to the touch (get an adult to help you). Remove from the oven and stand for 2 minutes. Dust with icing sugar. Serve puddings immediately topped with a dollop of cream and a spoonful of orange zest and syrup.

MY SCORE   /10

I really love a good Jaffa mousse, and this is the perfect consistency – you've done a really lovely job.

GARY MEHIGAN

MY SCORE 65 /10

Siena's
Jaffa Mousse

SERVES 4
PREPARATION 15 MINS
COOKING 5 MINS

You need to allow 3 hours for the mousse to set.

100g dark chocolate, chopped
40g unsalted butter
1 tsp orange zest, plus 1 tbs orange juice
1 tbs blood orange juice*
1 egg, separated
125ml (½ cup) thickened cream
2 tbs icing sugar

Citrus salad

1 orange
1 blood orange*
1 mandarin

Orange cream

125ml (½ cup) thickened cream
1 tsp icing sugar
1 tsp orange zest

STEP 1 Place chocolate and butter in a heatproof bowl set over a saucepan of barely simmering water (don't let bowl touch water). Stir until melted. Remove from heat (get an adult to help you). Stir in orange zest, orange juices and egg yolk until combined.
STEP 2 Using an electric mixer, beat cream to soft peaks. Fold into chocolate.
STEP 3 Using an electric mixer, whisk egg whites until firm peaks form, add icing sugar and whisk until thick and glossy. Fold half the whites into chocolate mixture, then gently fold in the remainder. Spoon mixture into 4 x 125ml (½ cup) ramekins and place in refrigerator for 3 hours or until set.
STEP 4 For citrus salad, peel and segment oranges (see Lesson #26, page 129). Using the bridge technique (see Lesson #2, page 7), cut the zest into strips. Peel and segment the mandarin. Combine fruits and zest in a small bowl.
STEP 5 For the orange cream, using an electric mixer, whisk cream and icing sugar until soft peaks form. Fold in zest.
STEP 6 Serve mousse with the citrus salad and orange cream.
✳ Blood oranges are from selected greengrocers; substitute regular oranges.

ABOUT SIENA

Siena, nine, from Victoria, sure has a way with desserts. From citrus curd tarts to this wicked choc-orange mousse, Siena's sweets have impressed the judges. "Siena's presentation was lovely and her mousse was perfect," said Anna Gare. "I haven't tasted one this good in quite some time."

Well I have to say this is gorgeous – raspberry and white chocolate should get married!

ANNA GARE

MY SCORE   /10

Sam's
Pound Cakes with Chocolate Shards

SERVES 4
PREPARATION 50 MINS
COOKING 15 MINS

130g unsalted softened
   butter, plus extra,
   to grease
150g (⅔ cup) caster sugar
1 tsp vanilla extract
2 eggs
150g (1 cup) plain flour
2 tsp baking powder
220g white chocolate,
   chopped
125ml (½ cup) thickened,
   cream, whipped
125g punnet raspberries
Icing sugar, to dust

STEP 1 Preheat oven to 170C. Lightly grease 4 holes of a Texas (180ml) muffin pan. Line a tray with baking paper.
STEP 2 Using an electric mixer, beat the butter, sugar and vanilla together in a large bowl until pale and fluffy. Add the eggs, one at a time, beating well after each addition. Sift the flour and baking powder over the egg mixture, then, using a wooden spoon, gently fold into the mixture until combined.
STEP 3 Spoon the mixture into the prepared pans and bake for 15 minutes or until a skewer inserted into the centre comes out clean. Cool in the pans for 5 minutes, then transfer to a wire rack to cool completely.
STEP 4 Meanwhile, place chocolate in a heatproof bowl set over a pan of just-simmering water (don't let the bowl touch the water), then stir until melted (get an adult to help you). Using a palette knife, spread the melted chocolate over the lined tray to 2mm thick. Refrigerate for 30 minutes until set.
STEP 5 Using a dinner knife, spread the cream over the top of the cakes. Break the chocolate into shards and arrange on top of the cakes with the raspberries. Dust with icing sugar, then serve.

ABOUT SAM

Eleven-year-old Sam, from Queensland, wasn't afraid to try some tricky techniques in the Top 50, tempering chocolate to use as a decoration for his pound cakes. These cakes are also known as quatre quarts, meaning 'four quarters in French, as the four ingredients in the original recipe are used in equal quantities. "I love the fact that you tempered chocolate," said George Calombaris. "You've created a lovely dessert – well done buddy!"

about
FRUIT

LESSON 25
How to peel & chop a mango

* Place mango on a chopping board. Using a sharp knife, cut down one side of the stone – if you feel some resistance you are too close to the stone, so shift the knife slightly. Repeat on the other side to form 2 cheeks.
* To peel, hold mango cheek in your hand, skin-side down. Slide a large spoon under the flesh and scoop it out.
* To cut mango cubes, place mango cheek on a board, skin-side down, and carefully cut through the flesh in a criss-cross pattern, taking care not to cut through the skin. Push the skin into the flesh – the mango will pop open.

Chilled mango cubes make an awesome summer snack.

LESSON 27
Fanning strawberries

Place a strawberry on a board, with the leafy top facing away from you. Make four cuts from the top of the berry to the base, taking care not to cut through the top. Gently spread out the slices to create a fan.

LESSON 26
Segmenting & pitting

SEGMENTING AN ORANGE Place orange on a chopping board and slice off the top and base so it sits flat. Slice off the skin, then remove all of the white pith, following the curve of the orange. Holding the orange over a bowl, carefully slide your knife between the membrane walls toward the centre of the orange to release the juicy segments (get an adult to help you).

PITTING CHERRIES Using a cherry pitter or olive pitter, place the cherry in the pitter, then press to release the stone. If you don't have a cherry pitter, using a knife, cut a small slit in the side of the fruit. Open the slit slightly, then remove the stone. To prevent cherry juice splattering your clothes, try pitting the cherries inside a large plastic bag.

Strawberry & Raspberry Jelly

SERVES **4**
PREPARATION **20 MINS**
SETTING **8 HOURS**

250g punnet strawberries
125g punnet blueberries
125g punnet raspberries
2x 85g packets
    raspberry jelly
500ml (2 cups) apple juice

MY SCORE   /10

STEP 1

Preparing the berries

Rinse strawberries and blueberries under cold water. Using a knife, hull the strawberries (remove the green tops), then halve or quarter any large ones using the bridge technique (see Lesson #2, page 7). Divide half the strawberries, raspberries and blueberries equally among 4 x 125ml (½ cup) moulds or 2 x 250ml (1 cup) moulds.

Chef's tip Empty yoghurt containers make perfect jelly moulds.

STEP 2

Making the jelly

To make the jelly, put the kettle on to boil. Place 1 packet jelly crystals in a heatproof jug. When the kettle has boiled, ask an adult to pour over 250ml (1 cup) boiling water. Using a long-handled spoon, stir continuously until crystals dissolve. Add 250ml (1 cup) apple juice and stir well. Leave to cool for 10 minutes.

STEP 3

Filling the moulds

Pour the jelly mixture over the berries to half-fill each container – the berries will float to the surface. Cool completely. Transfer to a tray, then carefully place in the fridge for 2 hours or until set.

STEP 4

Setting the jellies

Remove the jellies from fridge and scatter with the remaining berries. Make up the second packet of jelly (see Step 2) and pour over jellies. Return to the fridge for a further 2 hours to set. To turn jellies out of moulds, carefully dip the base of the mould into a bowl of hot water for a few seconds (get an adult to help you). Lift the mould out onto a tea towel and dry the bottom. Place a plate upside-down on top of the mould, then quickly turn the plate over so the mould is the right way up. The jelly should plop out neatly and be ready to eat.

Tutti frutti

You can really use your imagination with your jellies and add all sorts of fruit, such as orange, peaches, passionfruit, mango, grapes and lychees. Just steer clear of pineapple, kiwifruit and pawpaw, as these contain a special enzyme that prevents the gelatine from setting.

Mango Ice Blocks

SERVES **6**
PREPARATION **15 MINS**
FREEZING **4 HOURS**

6 ice-cream moulds
   or empty yoghurt
   containers
2 mangoes, chopped (see
   Lesson #25, page 129)
250ml (1 cup) mango
   and orange juice,
   plus extra to top up,
   if needed
6 paddle pop sticks

STEP 1
Measuring your moulds
Measure your moulds
by pouring water into
the empty moulds. Pour
water into a measuring jug
and note the amount.

STEP 1
Preparing the mango
Place the chopped mango
in a bowl and mash well
with a potato masher until
smooth. Add the juice and
stir until combined. Transfer
the mango mixture to a
jug. Top up with extra juice
if necessary, so you have
enough to fill 6 moulds.

STEP 2
Filling the moulds
Carefully pour the mango
mixture into the moulds,
leaving a 1cm gap at the
top (see Chill Out, below).
Insert paddle pop sticks,
leaving 4cm exposed to
use as a handle. Freeze
for 4 hours or until frozen.
To unmould the ice blocks,
briefly dip the moulds in
hot water to help ease
them out (get an adult
to help you).

CHILL OUT
When liquid freezes,
it expands as the water
turns to ice. To make
sure your ice blocks
don't overflow, always
leave a gap at the top
when filling your moulds.

MY SCORE   /10

Lemon Curd Ice-Cream & Mixed Berry Compote

MAKES **1 LITRE**
PREPARATION **20 MINS**
FREEZING **6 HOURS**

1 lemon
350g jar lemon curd*
500g Greek-style yoghurt
300ml thickened cream
500g (2 punnets)
   strawberries
125g (1 punnet) raspberries
2 tbs caster sugar
½ orange, juiced

MY SCORE   /10

STEP 1

Grating the lemon zest

Using a box grater, hold the top of the grater firmly with one hand. With your other hand, hold the lemon at the top end of the grater and push down the side of the grater with the smallest holes – try to avoid grating the bitter white pith. Using a pastry brush, remove the zest from the grater, then place in a bowl with the lemon curd and yoghurt.

STEP 2

Preparing the ice-cream

Pour the cream into a large bowl. Using an electric mixer, whisk the cream to soft peaks. Using a spatula, gently fold the whipped cream into the lemon curd mixture. Pour into a shallow plastic container, then cover and freeze for 6 hours or until firm. Take the ice-cream out of the freezer to soften for 10 minutes before serving.

STEP 3

Preparing the berries

Rinse the strawberries under cold water. Using a knife, hull the strawberries (remove the green tops), then halve or quarter any large ones using the bridge technique (see Lesson #2, page 7). Place strawberries, raspberries, sugar and orange juice in a saucepan over low heat. Cook, stirring, for 4 minutes or until sugar dissolves.

STEP 4

Making the compote

Using a ladle, remove half the berries and place in a bowl (get an adult to help you). Mash with a potato masher to a thick purée. Return purée to pan of whole berries. Cook over low heat for 3 minutes or until thickened slightly. Remove from heat and cool. Serve with ice-cream.
＊From supermarkets and specialist food shops.

Serve with a drizzle of passionfruit for a super-tangy treat.

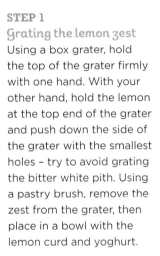

SWEET SENSATION

Compote is an easy fruit sauce that's great with ice-cream, scones and pancakes. If the fruit is ripe and juicy, you may not need to add sugar, so taste your fruit before you get started. You can use a mixture of raspberries, strawberries, blueberries and blackberries, or thawed frozen berries when they're not in season.

Masterclass with Poh
Yoghurt Panna Cottas with Raspberry Jelly

SERVES 6
PREPARATION 20 MINS
COOKING 20 MINS

You will need to allow an extra 4 hours for the panna cottas to set.

150g punnet raspberries
30g caster sugar
6 x gold-strength gelatine
   leaves
375ml (1½ cups) pouring
   cream
50g icing sugar, sifted
180g Greek-style yoghurt
1 tsp vanilla bean paste

Pistachio tuile
65g plain flour
65g icing sugar
65g softened butter
2 egg whites
50g pistachios,
   finely chopped

STEP 1
Making raspberry jelly
Combine the raspberries, caster sugar and 100ml water in a heatproof bowl. Place the bowl over a saucepan of simmering water for 5 minutes, stirring occasionally, so the raspberry flavour infuses the water. Meanwhile, soak 3 gelatine leaves in a bowl of cold water for 3 minutes or until soft. Squeeze out excess water. Add the gelatine to the raspberry mixture. Stir to dissolve gelatine. Strain jelly through a sieve into a jug (get an adult to help), reserving the raspberries. Spoon 4 raspberries into the base of each 6 x 125ml (½ cup) plastic dariole moulds, then divide the jelly mixture among the moulds. Refrigerate for 15 minutes or until set.

STEP 2
Making the panna cottas
Place cream and icing sugar in a small saucepan and stir over medium heat for 5 minutes or until heated through. Remove from heat. Soak remaining gelatine in cold water for 3 minutes or until soft, squeeze out excess water, then stir gelatine into cream mixture to dissolve. Gently whisk vanilla and yoghurt into cream until combined. Pour evenly over jelly in moulds, then refrigerate for 4 hours or until set.

STEP 3
Making the tuiles
Preheat oven to 160C. Sift flour and icing sugar into the bowl of a food processor. Add butter and egg whites, cover with the lid, then process until smooth. Refrigerate for 10 minutes or until chilled.

STEP 4
Baking the tuiles
Line 2 oven trays with baking paper, then trace 18 x 6cm rounds onto the trays. Using a spatula, spread 1 tsp tuile mixture to cover rounds. Sprinkle with pistachios, then bake each tray for 5 minutes or until light golden on the edges. Carefully remove from oven (get an adult to help you), then, using a spatula, immediately place the tuille onto a rolling pin and allow to cool to shape.

STEP 5
Serving panna cottas
Dip panna cottas in warm water for a few seconds to loosen. Carefully slide a paring knife around the inside edge of the mould, then invert moulds onto plates and gently shake to remove panna cotta. Serve with tuiles to the side.

MY SCORE   /10

Masterclass with George
Three Flavours of Granitas

Chinotto & kaffir lime granita
SERVES **6–8**
PREPARATION **20 MINS**
SETTING **45 MINS**

400ml Vittoria Chinotto*
1 tbs lemon juice
110g (½ cup) caster sugar
3 kaffir lime leaves

Combine all ingredients and 100ml water in a small pan and bring to the boil over medium–high heat. Reduce the heat to low–medium and simmer, stirring, for 10 minutes or until sugar dissolves. Remove from heat and cool. Pour the mixture into a shallow 18cm x 28cm tray. Place in the freezer for 45 minutes or until almost set. Remove from the freezer and, using a fork, scrape the ice into flakes. Serve immediately.
✳ A bitter Italian soda, available from delis.

Raspberry granita
SERVES **6–8**
PREPARATION **20 MINS**
SETTING **45 MINS**

2 x 125g punnet raspberries
165g (¾ cup) caster sugar
1 tbs lemon juice

Combine all ingredients and 500ml (2 cups) water in a small saucepan. Bring to the boil over medium–high heat. Reduce the heat to low–medium and simmer, stirring, for 10 minutes or until sugar dissolves. Remove from heat and cool. Purée raspberry mixture in a food processor, then strain through a fine sieve into a bowl. Discard seeds. Pour mixture into a shallow 18cm x 28cm tray and place in the freezer for 45 minutes or until almost set. Remove from the freezer and, using a fork, scrape the ice into flakes. Serve immediately.

Orange-flower granita
SERVES **6–8**
PREPARATION **20 MINS**
SETTING **45 MINS**

350ml orange juice
1 orange, zested
55g (¼ cup) caster sugar
1½ tbs lemon juice
3 drops orange-flower water*

Combine all ingredients and 150ml water in a small pan and bring to the boil over medium–high heat. Reduce the heat to low–medium and simmer, stirring, for 10 minutes or until sugar dissolves. Remove from heat and cool. Pour into a shallow 18cm x 28cm tray and freeze for 45 minutes or until almost set. Remove from the freezer and, using a fork, scrape the ice into flakes. Serve immediately.
✳ From Middle Eastern and specialist food stores.

MY SCORE   /10

SUBSCRIBE TO MASTERCHEF MAGAZINE – SAVE UP TO 30%

Celebrate the joy of cooking with **MasterChef Magazine**. Keep up to date with your favourite foodies, discover great recipes and pick up loads of tips and tricks from the experts with a monthly dose of Australia's hottest food magazine.

2 years (22 issues) for $76 – save 30%
1 year (11 issues) for $40 – save 27%

To subscribe, visit **magsonline.com.au/masterchef/X505**
or call **1300 656 933** and quote **X505**

WHY SUBSCRIBE?

* **Save on the cover price** – pay as little as $3.45 an issue

* **Free delivery** to your home

* **Never** miss an issue

* **A perfect gift** that lasts all year

Cooking notes

Baking All oven temperatures are for conventional, non-fan-forced ovens.

Chocolate Cocoa solids give chocolate its flavour. Dark chocolate has a higher percentage of cocoa solids than milk chocolate. Choose from 65% to 85%, depending on how bitter you like it. Avoid chocolate with added butter or oil, as it's not suitable for cooking.

Cream We've used three main types in our recipes. Pouring cream (35% butter fat) is also labelled as pure cream. Thickened cream (35% butter fat) contains gelatine and is most suitable for whipping. Double cream (48% butter fat or more) is usually for serving.

Eggs We recommend using eggs laid by free-range poultry. Use eggs at room temperature. Unless specified, all eggs used are 59g (extra large).

Grinding & crushing If you don't have a mortar and pestle, use the small bowl of a food processor. Or seal spices in a plastic bag and bash them with a rolling pin or the flat side of a meat mallet.

Lemons When serving wedges with dishes, cut them into wedges or 'cheeks'. To cut cheeks, cut the lemon lengthwise each side of the core.

Lemon juice When the flesh of some fruits, such as apples, pears and bananas, is exposed to air, it oxidises, resulting in discolouration. This can be slowed by adding lemon juice.

Onions We've used these varieties. Onions refer to the brown variety. Red onions are also called Spanish onions. Spring onions are the long, thin green variety. Eschalots are the small sweet variety with golden-coloured skin. Asian red eschalots are the small sweet variety with pinky-red skin available from Asian grocers.

Seafood & meat We recommend using free-range chickens and humanely reared pork. When cooking large cuts of meat, use a meat thermometer to measure the internal temperature of the meat to avoid under or overcooking.

Seasoning Unless stated otherwise, 'season' means to season with salt and pepper.

Vanilla We use three types of vanilla in our recipes. Vanilla essence is usually vanilla that has been artificially derived in an alcoholic base. There are a few Australian companies, including Queen, that produce natural vanilla essence. Vanilla extract is an extract from vanilla beans in an alcoholic base. Vanilla bean paste is derived from vanilla beans. 1 tsp vanilla bean paste is the flavour equivalent of the scraped seeds of 1 vanilla bean. Queen produces economical 65g jars of blended vanilla bean seeds in a natural syrup to give the flavour and look of real vanilla. Vanilla bean is vanilla in its purest form. To extract vanilla, split the bean lengthwise and scrape seeds.

Weights & sizes For accuracy, it's better to weigh ingredients rather than use cup measurements. Fruits and vegetables are medium-sized unless specified.

Index

V = vegetarian

MasterChef
MAGAZINE

Editor-in-Chief Trudi Jenkins
Managing Editor Sally Feldman
Food Director Sophia Young
Creative Director Scott Cassidy
Project Art Director Jacqui Porter
Project Editor Sarah Lewis
Photographer Jeremy Simons
Series Photographer Stuart Bryce
Stylist Amber Keller
Project Food Editor Julie Ballard
Project Food Preparation Daniel Taplin
Production Director Mark Moes
Production Manager Neridah Burke
Editorial Coordinator Kate Skinner
Editorial Enquiries (02) 8062 2791,
masterchef@newsmagazines.com.au
Group Publisher, Food Fiona Nilsson
Chief Executive Officer Sandra Hook

Contributors Stephanie Alexander, Steve Brown, George Calombaris,
Anna Gare, Amanda Grant, Yael Grinham, Poh Ling Yeow,
Gary Mehigan, Mark Roper, Dominic Smith

Stephanie Alexander's Bacon & Egg Pie (page 24)
reprinted from *The Cook's Companion* (Penguin/Lantern)
with permission from Stephanie Alexander

Thanks
All meat supplied by Hudson Meats (hudsonmeats.com.au)
All fruit and vegetables supplied by Velluti's (vellutis.com.au)
Small appliances supplied by Sunbeam (sunbeam.com.au)
Cake tins supplied by World Kitchen (worldkitchen.com.au)
Bowls and utensils supplied by VGM International (vgmimports.com.au)